Developing Play and Drama in Children with Autistic Spectrum Disorders

Dave Sherratt and Melanie Peter

David Fulton Publishers
London

David Fulton Publishers Ltd
Ormond House, 26–27 Boswell Street, London WC1N 3JZ

www.fultonpublishers.co.uk

First published in Great Britain in 2002 by David Fulton Publishers

Note: The right of Dave Sherratt and Melanie Peter to be identified as the authors of this work has been asserted by them in accordance with the Copyright, Designs and Patents Act 1988.

Copyright © 2002 Dave Sherratt and Melanie Peter

British Library Cataloguing in Publication Data
A catalogue record for this book is available from the British Library.

ISBN 1 85346 697 2

Typeset by Textype Typesetters, Cambridge
Printed and bound in Great Britain by The Cromwell Press, Trowbridge, Wilts.

Contents

For Charlie

(not forgetting his big brothers, Jesse and Sam!)

M.P.

For the late T. D. Sherratt

(my father and mentor)

D.S.

Acknowledgements

This book would not have happened without the support and cooperation of certain key people. We'd like to thank them all – professionals and people in our personal lives – for recognising the potential significance of our work for children with autism.

Dave Sherratt would like to acknowledge the assistance and huge support of the staff and children of Mowbray School and the other North Yorkshire schools that have been invaluable in this work. In particular, he would like to thank the Early Years and Autism Support staff. He would also like to express gratitude to the Teacher Training Agency, and particularly Cherry White and Philippa Cordingly for their support and research advice. Dave was aided in his work by the Greek Society for the Protection of Autistic People, particularly Vaya Papageorgiou, Yiannis Vogindroukas, Maria Goutziouli and Professor Christos Alexiou. There are a number of people that have not been included in the above who have, over a period of years, been inspirational. Dave owes a debt of thanks to Paul and Christine Shattock, Yakoub Islam, Carol Potter, Hilary Dinham, Elaine Williams, Jonathon Mitchell, Mick Connelly and, particularly, Gill Donald. Finally, without the support and understanding of his family, none of this work would have been possible. Dave would like to thank them and take them out for a celebration when this book is published.

Melanie Peter would like to express her appreciation for the enthusiasm of colleagues and, most especially, those children with autism with whom she has, over the years, shared a learning process. Thanks are extended as well to Suffolk College in Ipswich, and the Open University, for their continuing support for her research in this area. Judy Sebba and Mary James at the University of Cambridge Institute of Education have also played an influential role in Melanie's development as a practitioner and researcher; material in Appendix C is based on findings from her MEd thesis. In recent times, staff and pupils at Harford Manor School in

Norwich have demonstrated invaluable support for Melanie's work – thank you especially to Geoff Kitchen, Janice Wiggins and Green Class. Melanie would also like to express a personal indebtedness to the school, on behalf of her son Jesse, who has autism. He is a daily reminder that the approach proposed in this book works! This is credit also, to the commitment of other professionals, particularly those based at the Mill Lane bungalows, Aylsham, in Norfolk; likewise to friends who have persisted in playing with Jesse over the years, including Jean and Anna Mason, Donna Kelf, Jody Sexton and Valerie Davis. Additionally, and most especially, Jesse's progress is due to the dedication and resolve of all members of his family to reach and involve him – thank you, everyone. Melanie would also like to express her gratitude to them, for their everlasting patience and support over her work – not least in the writing of this book.

We'd both like to thank staff and students at the University of Birmingham, for all the stimulating debates and continuing interest in our innovations and the development of our approach as an intervention for autism. Rita Jordan, Glenys Jones and Tina Tilstone deserve particular mention. A formal expression of gratitude is due as well for kind permission to reproduce material from Distance Education documents for the Autism and Learning Difficulties modules (units on 'Access to the Curriculum' and 'The Arts', respectively). We also greatly appreciate the insights and support of academic staff involved in our respective PhD degrees at the University of Warwick and the University of East Anglia, in particular our tutors, Professors Jill Boucher and John Schostak.

Finally, we'd especially like to thank Tom Hunt for his support and for commenting so assiduously on the drafts – also for keeping us plied with wonderful refreshments!

Introduction

Something has always puzzled us during our 20 years in special education: why is it that educationalists know that children learn through play, yet seem to lose sight of this when it comes to children with special needs? This becomes even more of a paradox with children with autism, to the extent that 'work' and 'play' become totally separated in their perception. This book aims to redress this situation, and in so doing, seeks to improve the quality of their lives. We are also determined to put some fun back into education – children learn best when they are enjoying themselves, and teaching, too, becomes so much more pleasurable! It is important that our enthusiasm is not misconstrued: this book is not a 'cure for autism'; rather, we present play-drama intervention as a pragmatic approach to developing practice with 'hard to reach' children, that is compatible with current curricular contexts, and which touches the very core of the difficulties experienced by children with autism. There is a deeper debate at issue here.

We know through many years' experience that the practical strategies presented in this book *work*. However, we wish to challenge the orthodoxy, by inviting response to the underlying theoretical premise that is advanced here for our approach. Children with autism seem to lack a desire to search for deeper causal links in their understanding of the world. Instead they excel at remembering predictable routines (for example, teeth cleaning) and processing surface level information such as train timetables. This results in a fragmented and shallow understanding of the world, although they can remember lots about it. They need to find *causal coherence* through their experiences: how it is that events are connected as a result of action – *play* is the means that all children achieve this. The difficulties of children with autism become exacerbated and most noticeable in the area of social understanding, where they experience difficulty in making sense of the behaviour of other people because it relies on an understanding of their intentions. This can be addressed by extending their play further using techniques from educational *drama*, so that children with autism can be offered a reflective window on their own behaviour and that of others.

The very act of engaging in play and drama experiences will strengthen those parts of the brain that are under-functioning in children with autism. Play and drama evoke emotional reactions in children: putting children with autism directly in touch with their feeling responses will enable them to see how events and experiences come together to have a *meaning* – a personal significance – rather than just be related chronologically. This process needs to be made explicit to them, so that they may be led to appreciate their own mental states and those of others, and how these influence behaviour. In this way, they may gain greater social understanding. Play and drama also require children to think flexibly – a fundamental difficulty for those with autism. However, unless constructive intervention is put in place, this will remain a 'vicious circle' and a characterising impairment. Quite simply, children with autism only 'can't play' because they don't know how to play – and if they are not encouraged to play, then they won't be able to play!

The approach advocated here, play-drama intervention, requires a clear play structure to be presented, within which children with autism may gradually learn how to make creative decisions and choices within broadening boundaries. This book offers a developmental framework for play and drama, that leads children from tightly structured, predictable activities to more open-ended structures that may facilitate spontaneous pretend play. Drama-in-education harnesses children's make-believe, and enables the teacher to provide opportunities to explore implications of their actions and behaviour, and to understand directly their relevance to the real world. There is abundant psychological research that demonstrates powerfully the importance of children's developing symbolism, make-believe play and understanding of narrative for their subsequent *social competence*. If this is not to develop spontaneously in children with autism, then it will need to be explicitly taught – otherwise their life experiences will be necessarily more limited.

How are children with autism going to discover play unless we provide them with opportunities? It is not the case that children with autism 'can't play' – rather, it is the case that they frequently opt *not* to play, even though they may have latent play potential. This book seeks to demonstrate how it is possible to tap this ability through play-drama intervention, and enable children with autism to discover the inherent pleasure of engaging in such activity. By developing this in *social contexts* from the outset, this pleasure will come to be associated with other people, so convincing the child that there is 'something in it for them' to bother with others. This will help underpin progress in their communication and social interaction skills – and also their fundamental trust in other people. It will have a knock-on effect, too, in enabling them to embrace change. These faculties will also be enhanced through their growing ability to flex the mind and cope with the unexpected.

Chapter 1 presents a rationale for an approach through play and drama as an intervention for children with autism. It highlights the distinct cognitive dimensions as well as the affective (the latter being more commonly associated with 'playful' activity), and demonstrates how play-drama intervention offers an integrating way forward for children with autism. Crucially, play and drama experiences fulfil essential criteria for enabling children to flourish: as catalysts for unleashing ability; opportunities to be creative; and through being inherently motivating. Chapter 2 probes deeper into the play behaviour of children with autism and proposes a theoretical basis for the importance of play, with implications for practice. This premise is founded on the operation of two processes: first, the effect it may have on brain functioning, and second, the psychological fusion of children's interest and emotional engagement within a particular play sequence.

In Chapter 3, the role of the teacher in play-drama intervention is discussed, and a practical framework is offered for developing play in children with autism. If their play potential is to be tapped, then the disparity between their apparent and latent ability needs to be ascertained; assessment observation schedules are presented for both free-play and structured play contexts. A series of increasingly challenging play structures is explored, with examples from practice – Appendix A provides a wealth of further activities, with Appendix B also cross-referenced, containing additional examples for explicitly promoting social play. Chapter 4 offers a way of taking play into drama that is appropriate even for those at the earliest stages of learning. It presents a pivotal drama structure that inherently contains elements that teach children the language of make-believe – a 'learning how to do it while doing it' approach!

Chapters 5 and 6 delve into the drama process in more depth, to explore opportunities for children with autism in engaging in this kind of activity. Chapter 5 considers the way learning may be promoted through drama, and its usefulness as a teaching tool across the curriculum. It also highlights the specific ways in which drama can address the 'triad of impairments' experienced by children with autism, leading to improvements in flexible thinking, social interaction and communication. In Chapter 6, ways to engage children with autism meaningfully within the drama are described, with discussion of teaching strategies and drama conventions appropriate for different stages of their play development.

Chapter 7 offers suggestions for developing understanding of narrative – a key to social understanding. A model is presented to enable children with autism to access meanings embedded within stories: exploring key moments when players are under tension, with a problem or dilemma to be faced, in order to understand them and their subsequent impact. Drama can move children closer to an understanding of text; suggestions are offered for enabling children with autism to link the written word with meaning arising from human action. It also considers ways to develop their potential as 'playwrights', able to use play for a purpose – to communicate meaning.

Finally, a postscript summarises the value of play-drama intervention for children with autism, with specific references to the current statutory context. This is presented as a concluding rationale to support teachers in justifying play and drama in their timetables! Two further appendices offer additional useful material: Appendix C suggests guidelines for developing drama work (pointers for practice in relation to children with autism), and Appendix D lists resources for play. It should be noted that all practical examples are intended as a stimulus – springboards for teachers to develop their own practice, geared to the specific needs and interests of their particular children. They should be used as a starting-point, rather than an exact template.

To avoid clumsiness, the term 'teacher' is used throughout to indicate a player or organiser with superior playing or organisational ability, whose key role is to help the child with autism to extend his or her thinking abilities through play and drama. 'Teacher' is thus a generic term, to refer also to others involved generally in their education – teaching assistants, parents, carers, therapists, voluntary helpers, siblings or other children. Similarly, the term 'child with autism' is intended to refer to all those on the receiving end of such experiences, and will include those with autism, Asperger's syndrome, and a range of other disorders across the autistic spectrum.

Play-drama intervention is also relevant for adults with autism, with the important proviso that material is adapted and presented in a way that is dignified, and which acknowledges the player's actual age. Teachers working with children (and adults) with other designated special needs requiring step-by-step developmental programmes will also find this book helpful, including those with severe and profound and multiple learning difficulties. Similarly, children with a range of emotional and behavioural difficulties may benefit from the secure framework presented here that, at the same time, enables them to develop relationships and greater social understanding.

As the saying goes, 'consistency is the last refuge of the unimaginative'! This book aims to revitalise practice in relation to children with autism, that in recent years has tended to become dry and devoid of spirit, appealing to their rigidity of thought rather than to their creative potential. 'Consistency' has become such a buzz word, that their education seems to have lost sight of the value and importance of teaching them to embrace difference and to deal with new challenges creatively – especially in these fast-moving times. Children with autism are children, first and foremost, with a need and latent desire to play. Play-drama intervention can prepare children for life, enabling them to understand human interaction and to engage more effectively in a social world. It is our job to unlock this potential – and entitlement. . . It's fun too – enjoy!

Dave Sherratt and Melanie Peter
September 2001

CHAPTER 1

Why Play?

One morning recently, Charlie (the young son of one of the authors) initiated a short play sequence. He opened with a familiar piece of narration, lifted from *Teletubbies*, the popular children's TV programme: adopting a theatrical pose, he announced: 'One day in Teletubbyland, something appeared from far away: it was . . . a pair of shoes [he threw his mother's shoes in front of him, and cast her a quick knowing smile] . . . So, Charlie tried on the shoes . . . They were too big . . . [he sighed disappointedly] . . . And so Laa Laa tried on the shoes' [he reached for one of his Teletubby dolls and put her feet into the shoes]. At this point, Charlie paused; he seemed to realise the need for some kind of resolution to the situation . . . He resorted to a 'quick fix', the familiar format used in the TV programme: 'Suddenly, the shoes disappeared! [throwing the shoes back over his shoulder] . . . BIG HUG! [he gathered all four of his Teletubby dolls together] . . . BIG HUG, Mummy!' [drawing his mother into the game].

Charlie is just three years old, but already has a clear understanding of symbolism, of narrative structure, and a desire to personalise the experience and share meaning with others. He can invest affective elements (emotion) into his play, incorporate sequences drawn from memory, and flexibility and fluidity in the way he is able to manipulate them (here, varying and adding to the TV story). He uses speech to describe what is happening and to communicate to others, and the whole experience is highly interactive and socially oriented. One of his elder brothers, Jesse, similarly used to engage, seemingly, in make-believe when he was Charlie's age, and also delighted in lifting familiar themes from television. The difference, however, was that Jesse's play would become stuck. Jesse would lift chunks of text directly from *Postman Pat*, strutting about with an immaculately imitated Yorkshire accent, and fingers spread apart in the characteristic Postman Pat walk. However, his play did not develop beyond the memorised extract, and he resisted wildly any gentle attempt from anyone else to enter the make-believe, even though his mother could impersonate the character Mrs Goggins to a tee! Jesse has a diagnosis of autistic spectrum disorder.

So why play? Many parents would probably describe their frustration at *not* being able to engage their child with autism in purposeful play, and their child's obsessive interest in items that would not hold conventional intrinsic motivation for the majority – the hours spent twiddling string, for example. Yet those same parents might also mention some exceptions to isolated activity: their child's enjoyment of rough-and-tumble, chasing games and interest in adults' clowning around, slapstick, the incongruous and in frippery in general. They might also instance some tantalising glimpses of their child momentarily engaged in play similar to that of children without autism, but point out how this was only fleeting, and how their child seemed to lose interest quickly, and did not seem either to want to keep the activity going or know how to do so.

This book seeks to demonstrate how the worlds (real and imaginary) of children like Jesse and Charlie can be brought closer together. This chapter will provide a rationale for play-drama intervention a structured approach for children with autism that has play at its core, and that seeks not only to expand their repertoire of possibilities, but also to extend their understanding and use of their own play behaviour. It is the development of imagination, make-believe and narrative understanding in shared play contexts, that leads ultimately towards children's growing social competence. This chapter proposes a multi-factional model for developing play and taking it into educational drama, capitalising on opportunities for unleashing learning potential, possibilities for creativity and intrinsic motivational qualities.

Play and drama: unleashing ability

Arguably, play is at the core of what it is to be human. It is a long-established educational maxim, that children learn through play, however transformed that may become as they mature. Play as a process facilitates discovery of possibilities, allows for exploration and experimentation and offers practice opportunities to enhance and consolidate knowledge, skills and understanding. As such, there is a close association between 'playfulness' and a person's essential *creativity*, with play generally regarded as a fundamental element in the creative process. This notion really needs close probing, especially as children with autism are deemed fundamentally challenged in this area. Indeed, it is the indicators of their *rigidity of thought* – the very antithesis of creativity – that contribute to a diagnosis of 'autistic spectrum disorder', and which underpin the coincidence of related difficulties experienced in *communication* and *social interaction* – 'the triad of impairments' (Wing 1996).

Vygotsky (1978) claimed that 'in play a child always behaves beyond his average

age [because] play contains all developmental tendencies in a condensed form' (p. 241). For the majority of children with autism, it would seem that this 'playfulness' commonly remains latent: they seem to lack the urge to engage spontaneously in 'playful' behaviour in 'free-play' situations, while structured play contexts with an interested adult can reveal indications of their play potential and clear enjoyment of such activities. The tendency of many currently favoured approaches to working with children with autism is to by-pass their apparent shortcomings in play behaviour, and instead appeal to their cognitive, logical strengths, and to work *with* their tendency to rigidity of thought. Such 'compensatory' approaches, for example TEACCH (Teaching and Educating Autistic and Communication impaired Children – Schopler and Olley 1982) tend to be heavily directive, relying on highly explicit, visual structure and predictable organisation to minimise stress. Distinction is made between 'play' and 'work': children sit at individual 'work stations', with tasks presented in a dry, stimulus-free context, with a view to them learning to take greater responsibility for managing themselves, and with the minimum interaction to support successful completion of activities.

However, sometimes this would appear to risk being at the expense of a more holistic approach, not least the latent creative potential of children with autism, and the extent to which their essential playfulness may be compromised. It could be argued that making tasks devoid of interaction, risks children 'learning *equipment*', rather than addressing the potential of learning contexts for developing *relationships*, and discovering pleasure in human contact. Logic would seem to suggest that children experiencing difficulty in a particular area (in this case, play) should receive *more* support in it, not less! Ironically, however, a structured approach to teaching children with autism explicitly how to play creatively actually has an overtly *cognitive* dimension to it.

At the same time, play is essentially *affective* activity – an aspect of brain functioning that is problematic for children with autism. Children with autism are fundamentally challenged in their ability to encode and decode meaning (Frith 1989); they appear to demonstrate lack of empathy and have difficulty with flexible, lateral thinking, resulting in tendency to literal, logical modes of thought (see Figure 1.1). These difficulties may all stem from under-functioning of that part of the brain concerned with evaluation and affective activity (Damasio and Maurer 1978), which may hamper their ability to see significance and meaning in an experience, as well as undermine their sense of self and consequent awareness of other people (Jordan and Powell 1995). This difficulty with 'sense of self' and evaluating affective experience means that they struggle with understanding their own emotional states. It also prevents them from understanding how emotions are related to desires and beliefs, and therefore from empathising with other people's mental states and expression of intention – 'theory of mind' (Baron-Cohen 1993).

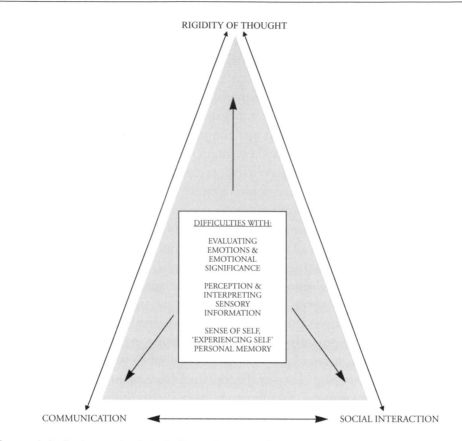

Figure 1.1 Autism – the 'triad of impairments' (based on Wing, 1996; Jordan and Powell, 1995)

However, activity that is inherently playful tends to generate *emotional* responses, and so will actually target directly that part of the brain that may be under-functioning in children with autism (Peter 2000b). Such experiences may also be more *memorable* because they are more highly charged (fun, exciting, pleasurable, intriguing – even annoying or frustrating), and therefore more likely to be etched on the brain due to their emotional quality: research has shown a link between emotional arousal in the mid-brain and cortical operations of thinking and problem-solving (Iveson 1996). Play-based approaches are live, energising and potentially liberating, and so tend to be affirming and reinforce a sense of self, which children with autism otherwise find difficult to achieve. Also, because play-based approaches are invariably *multi-sensory*, they offer potential points of contact in a range of ways, and so have in-built opportunities to access a shared meaning in an experience. This may be particularly significant for children with autism, who are known to perceive stimuli with heightened sensory awareness, and commonly have a preferred sensory mode.

Some people with autism are renowned for their outstanding artistic ability: the art of Stephen Wiltshire – celebrated for his drawings of buildings, Derek Paravacini's breathtaking music prowess and the lyrical poetry of the young boy Tito. While there are those (very few) with demonstrated exceptional creative ability, this book proposes that potential in *all* children with autism may be promoted by actually targeting areas of the brain that may be under-functioning. Through a 'remedial' approach that attempts simultaneously to activate areas of the brain associated with emotions and generative thought, it is possible to put children with autism in touch with their latent playfulness and 'what's in it for them', and *explicitly teach* them how to be creative in play and discover that potential. In other words, use a 'learning how to do it while doing it' approach!

Studies into the psychology of children's pretend play have evidenced the importance of *role playing* and *narrative* at the heart of socialisation and learning to be part of a culture. Vygotsky (1978) recognised that play enables children to learn cultural tools (such as turn-taking, queuing and conversational skills) through the facilitation of adults and/or peers. He also recognised how play activities based on real-life and domestic scenarios enable children to internalise socio-cultural conventions and also transcend them as they extend them and make them their own. It is clear that without intervention, impairments experienced by children with autism in communication, social interaction and flexible thinking will undermine their real potential play competence and subsequent development. This is apparent through examining the following research findings cited by Faulkner (1995) and Jordan (1999).

Make believe

Fein (1984) noted how through make-believe, children in role develop the ability to acknowledge and understand the perspectives of others as well as their own. Sachs *et al.* (1985) claim that children's development in creating and sustaining roles and themes in their *socio-dramatic play* is related to: firstly, their knowledge of scripted events (people engaged in purposeful activity that involves sequences of actions, such as bathing a baby), and secondly, their communicative competence. Research by Nelson (1986) supports this view, with evidence that this script knowledge is acquired through repeated observation and participation in such everyday activities, which becomes more elaborate over time. In order to use this script knowledge effectively however, children have to be able to convey their ideas to one another, negotiate shared meanings, and agree roles, play context and the evolving story line. Children with autism tend not to learn 'by osmosis', simply through exposure to situations in their environment: their inability to perceive meaning mitigates against purposeful involvement, both in the real world and in make-believe.

Other psychologists distinguish between children's socio-dramatic play and *themed fantasy play.* Corsaro (1986) highlighted how language in themed fantasy play tends to be more creative and flexible; Singer and Singer (1990) also observed how children's fantasy play is often highly original and imaginative. They contend that themed fantasy play (more than socio-dramatic play) enables children to play out and come to terms with important emotional tensions and themes. They map the distinction between children's socio-dramatic pretend play and themed fantasy play onto Bruner's (1986) distinction between different modes of thinking, and propose that the two types of play have different functions in terms of the holistic development of children's imagination and thought processes. According to this conceptualisation, socio-dramatic play echoes Bruner's *paradigmatic* mode of thinking: it is logical, sequential and analytical, involving ordering and categorising of events as children make sense of experience. By contrast, themed fantasy play echoes Bruner's *narrative* mode of thought, as it is more creative, expressive and entails construction of real or imagined events.

The implication is that both socio-dramatic and themed fantasy play may contribute to children's holistic development of social competence, but if children with autism are to access both paradigmatic and narrative modes of thought in this way, then they will need to be explicitly taught. Bruner and Feldman (1993) suggest that the failure of narrative ability and consequent difficulty in 'cultural framing' in children with autism, prevents them from organising their experience into forms by which others regulate their sociality, and go as far as to propose this theory as an explanation for autism; Jordan (1999) has highlighted the paucity of research to address this claim.

The studies of Leekam *et al.* (1997) suggest it is the lack of spontaneous gaze monitoring in autism that accounts for their failure to learn from others: 'if there is no shared attention, there can be no common topics for elaboration' (Jordan 1999: 106). Bruner and Feldman (1993) also draw attention to the difficulty experienced by children with autism in mutual imitation with a carer, and how in contrast, early interactions with normally developing children have a familiar characteristic 'narrative' shape to them, from which they generalise representations to other contexts. For example, a peek-a-boo game involves:

1. mutual eye-gaze (establishing a play context);
2. carer hides face (deepening involvement, introducing tension – a problem or dilemma);
3. carer reveals face (striving to resolve the situation);
4. 'boo!' (a climactic outcome is reached).

Other research evidence into the significance of narrative for the development of children *without* autism provides further insights.

Narrative

Whitehead (1997) considers narrative to be fundamental for children's development, and contends that narrating seems strongly linked to the organisation and recall of memory. She claims that children possess an innate drive to tell stories about an event, person or feeling, and an associated urge to evaluate and make judgements about them 'in order to give meaning and significance to the endless stream of sensations and events' (p. 90). 'This re-presentation of experiences in order to understand them better is a marked feature of human thinking, occurring in children's play, in art, and across cultures' (Whitehead 1997: 90)

Gregory (1977) proposes that narrative actually may have evolutionary significance, and that 'brain fictions' – hypotheses about the possible outcomes of courses of action and sequences of events – enable us to generate scenarios of likely outcomes to situations and to rehearse how we might react and cope. Young children make early moral judgements in terms of powerful opposites found in stories (for example weak/strong, good/bad, happy/sad), according to the value system and beliefs shared by the prevailing culture of the community. Narrative is regarded as fundamental to a developing sense of self within a social world, not just as forming the foundations for the development of children's literacy: 'Narrative form is a turning-point in a human being's understanding both of the world and of themselves' (Jones 1996: 141).

It follows, that if children with autism are unfamiliar with narratives through lack of participation in the social practices in which these narratives originate, they will become alienated from their social world, and withdraw from communicative contexts (Jordan 1999). This inability to recognise and use narrative structure may underpin their pragmatic difficulties in using language effectively (Baron-Cohen 1988), and impairment in commenting on or communicating novel information (Tager-Flusberg 1993).

The premise underpinning play-drama intervention rests on the implication from all the aforementioned research: a need for greater awareness of the potential significance of imaginative play and narrative development for children with autism. All the above evidence would seem to point to the need for a structured approach to developing and extending imaginative play that enables children with autism ultimately to harness narrative. A plausible approach is to devise structured contexts in which to teach them a rudimentary ability to play, and to combine this with practices used in drama-in-education that will enable them to gain an objective 'handle' on its significance.

Booth (1994) claims that the speculative nature of role-playing develops children's ability to think creatively, to examine the many levels of meaning that underlie each action; he sees *drama-in-education* as an extension of spontaneous role play in early childhood, and that such experiences are formative in facilitating their understanding of narrative and subsequent literacy development. Neelands (2000) similarly claims that through drama-in-education, it is possible for children to engage with narrative (including established texts) in a meaningful way that feeds directly from their everyday realities and concerns.

All drama takes human experience as its subject matter, in order to illuminate aspects of human behaviour in analogous situations. Drama-in-education seeks to take children's make-believe into areas of learning through structured play situations, in order to confront and explore implicit meanings. This can be through challenging children's own developing narrative, or bringing an established text alive. Children make connections between the fictitious context and the real world, and in this way are enabled to reflect on why people think and behave as they do. Drama-in-education also explicitly teaches children how to engage with material through developing their understanding and use of the art form: how meanings may be constructed using the theatre form, and similarly in the real world (for example, use of language, social space between people, symbolic use of objects, etc.).

In drama, cultural symbols and metaphors are harnessed – played around with – to encapsulate meanings (ideas, thoughts and feelings) in narrative – visually, aurally and kinaesthetically, not just in the spoken or written word. In turn, this statement may be presented to others in the form of a scripted or improvised play. As an audience, we endeavour to appreciate how a piece has been constructed in order to convey a message, and so access the meaning(s) embedded in the play. Drama is an art form, and contains *expression* of meanings (ideas, thoughts and feelings) in a range of forms; drama may also (but not necessarily) involve *communication* of feeling responses to an audience. Perhaps it is not surprising that many children with autism become 'switched on' by drama: drama involves making and sharing meanings as an essentially *cognitive* process (see Figure 1.2).

Drama-in-education also offers children with autism the opportunity to address head-on their fundamental difficulty with *affective* experience (Peter 2000b). It offers opportunities to put children with autism directly in touch with their feeling responses and those of others, and to channel and make sense of them with an awareness of their own mental state and those of others (see Figure 1.2). Grove and Park (2001) highlight how many individuals with learning difficulties find it hard to comprehend mental states, and possible discrepancies between what people do, and what they think and feel, and the particular value of drama to them for exploring 'theory of mind'. Drama-in-education also teaches children explicitly about narrative, and offers the potential to children with autism for exploring – and enjoying – an additional *aesthetic* dimension, so that play may become a means to an end, not just an end in itself.

'Aesthetic' literally means 'knowing through the senses' (Witkin 1974); with this

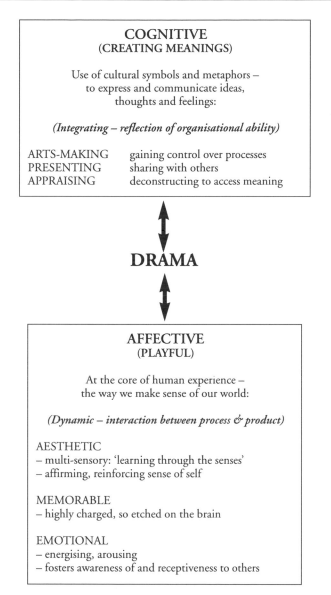

Figure 1.2 Drama and autism

at its heart, this book proposes play-drama intervention as an approach for working with children with autism that is the very antithesis of being *an*aesthetic!

Playfulness and creativity

Why bother? Duffy (1998) claims that *all* children need to represent their experiences, their feelings and ideas if they are to preserve them and share them with others:

> By encouraging creativity and imagination we are promoting children's ability to explore and comprehend their world and increasing their opportunities to make new connections and reach new understandings . . . Through their imagination children can move from the present into the past and the future, to what might be and beyond. (p. 8)

Arguably, the development of children's intuitive thought has been compromised for the sake of greater value set on logical and systematic thought (Bruner 1986; Duffy 1998). This is exemplified to an extreme in the case for children with autism, where popular highly directive approaches such as TEACCH, supported by the general orthodoxy, have tended to appeal to their cognitive strengths at the expense of more holistic, child-centred approaches. Yet in a rapidly changing, fast moving and culturally diverse world, if children with autism are to be able to cope with – and embrace – the unexpected and unforeseen, and to have dealings with a diversity of people, then their capacity for creative, flexible, imaginative thinking needs to be developed.

Play lies at the core of a person's essential creative and imaginative output (Moyles 1989), and as indicated above, is integral to the whole creative process: 'play promotes the flexibility and problem-solving skills that are needed to be creative' (Duffy 1998: 23). A critical notion will be recognition by the teacher of a child's genuine creative response, both within structured play contexts, and in informal, open-ended activity. What is it that we are actually seeking to promote through structured play and drama opportunities, that would seem to be the missing element in the play behaviour of children with autism in spontaneous, open-ended contexts? '[The creative process] involves a condensation of perceptual information and its transformation into a new form' (McKellar 1957; cited in Duffy 1998: 76). It is important to scrutinise what we mean by 'creativity', so that indicators may be identified, and the emergence of more spontaneous play behaviours tracked.

A creative response does not have to result in something startlingly original! Rather, the significant factor is the act of creating: coming up with new ideas or products, or recombining existing ones, in a way that is novel and meaningful to the person concerned (Gallagher 1985). The National Advisory Committee on Creative and Cultural Education (NACCCE), chaired by Ken Robinson, offered the following definition of creativity: 'Imaginative activity fashioned so as to produce outcomes that are both original and of value' (DfEE 1999: 29).

The NACCCE (DfEE 1999) expand on four characteristics of creative processes: imagination, pursuing a purpose, originality and the notion of value.

Imagination

Imagination involves 'internalising our perceptions, and using them and objects to create meanings that do not depend on the external world' (Duffy 1998: 20). It may be considered as 'a capacity to explore and experiment with memory, and to combine ideas rationally or irrationally' (Peter 1996a: 5). This begs the question of having something to remember; it is the teacher's responsibility to feed that imagination by providing a store of experiences on which to draw – visual, aural and tactile. Creative responses may be not just to a stimulus within a particular activity, but also to a particular technique involved, or to the materials and equipment themselves. Appealing to the full range of senses in children with autism will maximise their chances of engaging with an experience – they often appear to have a preferred sensory mode. A multi-sensory approach will also reinforce a greater 'sense of self', and their awareness – and memory – of their involvement in an experience. Additionally however, children with autism will need support in accessing their memory through objects of reference and other visual cues.

Children with autism appear to experience difficulty in the spontaneous drive or motivation to discover play possibilities for themselves, even though actually they may be capable of undergoing the cognitive processes that will move them to a new stage of development. Without an apparent impulse to play, it follows that creativity may be perceived differently by the person with autism (Aylott and Rickard 2001). Grandin (1997) comments how she distinguishes between thoughts and emotion, and Schneider (1999), another adult with autism, claims it is possible to understand artistic expression as a fusion of thought and feeling, without direct emotional engagement or empathy. However, Williams (1996) relates how early musical experiences did affect her emotionally and enabled her to express feelings, albeit somewhat disconnected from her conscious control and perception.

Structured activities will be crucial in order to demonstrate possibilities (whether involving equipment, materials or ideas) to children with autism, if necessary explained step-by-small-step, and to provide them with sufficient space and practice time to play. While this may seem very prescriptive, paradoxically it may enable children with autism to expand their fund of ideas, and gain control over certain procedures or 'play scripts', and to use this mastery to make new connections. The proviso is that they then need to be provided with opportunities to use their newfound mastery of play possibilities in open-ended contexts, where they may then make informed creative choices towards an original outcome.

However, it is important to remain open at all stages of an activity to additional, spontaneous child-led possibilities, and encourage children with autism to explore, experiment and elaborate. George (1992) identifies various possible kinds of creative indicators at different stages of an activity:

- *fluency of thought* (coming up with alternatives, solutions);
- *flexibility of thought* (shifting types of thinking, considering several approaches);
- *originality* (unusual, unique possibilities);

- *elaboration* (developing, improving, changing).

Similarly, the NACCCE (DfEE 1999) liken imagination to mental play, a *generative* mode of thought in which we attempt to:

- expand possibilities;
- look at a situation from a new perspective;
- combine or reinterpret ideas in different ways;
- apply ideas in new situations;
- make unusual connections, analogies or see new relationships.

Critics argue that the outstanding drawing of Stephen Wiltshire, while demonstrating impeccable draughtsmanship, is essentially a function of photographic memory. His more recent work as an adult, however, indicates development in terms of greater interpretative quality, and exploration with colour and with paint as a medium; nowadays he can be highly articulate, and is able to talk confidently to others. This is remarkable progress, as he still did not speak at the age of 11, when he first became widely known. It could be claimed that nurturing his extraordinary ability over the years has facilitated his growing social competence, not just the development of his artistic creativity from his original rigid style: encouraging him to 'play' has supported associated gains in more lateral, flexible thinking, and communication and social interaction skills.

Purpose

Creativity also implies a sense of *purpose* (NACCCE, DfEE 1999), although this may emerge in process – or even after the activity – so that the eventual outcome perhaps differs from that anticipated at the outset. Both the child with autism and the teacher may be challenged by an unanticipated turn of events; both need to learn to capitalise on spontaneous opportunities! Reminding the child with autism of the ultimate goal of an activity and redirecting them towards the quest, may facilitate a more positive response and creative attitude to embrace the possibility of dealing with change. The implication is that creativity entails a dynamic process, towards solving some central issue or problem and this may appeal to the cognitive strengths of children with autism. However, they will need to be enabled to develop more flexible thinking through carefully paced decisions between gradually broadening boundaries, from clear-cut, concrete, tangible choices, ultimately perhaps to more abstract ideas. Being creative involves active engagement, deliberation and a sense of intentionality, even though there may be moments of intuition along the way and a true sense of purpose perhaps only emerges afterwards (as in the case of a representational use ascribed to a structure made from found sources).

For certain children with autism, this sense of purpose may be emergent. It may be a case of discovering a sense of purpose through the playful activity itself, although this is likely to be more meaningful if a clear goal is presented to the child; he or she may not perceive the point of an activity otherwise. This is not to suggest that a child should be required to copy exactly an exemplar (such as imitating a play action identically to the teacher) – indeed, a truly creative response would then be regarded as a mistake! Rather, that the teacher should make the point of the activity clear to the child, and then 'scaffold' an individually tailored route (Wood et al. 1976). In this way, the gap may be bridged between a child's present spontaneous play behaviour as observed in free-play, open-ended contexts, and the potential levels of development revealed in structured play situations (Vygotsky 1978).

When scaffolding children's learning, adults need to:

- be finely tuned to the children's ability;
- provide a flexible framework and be aware of where children may be heading;
- respond to and follow up remarks and comment from children.

(Duffy 1998: 94)

Gradually, over time, it may be possible to discern the extent to which the child with autism may be demonstrating a growing sense of purpose within an experience, progressing from an initial encounter within an activity to creative achievement:

- *encounter* – tolerating being present, being provided with sensations;
- *awareness* – noticing that something is going on;
- *response* – showing surprise, enjoyment, dissatisfaction;
- *engagement* – directed attention, focused looking, listening, showing interest, recognition, recall, sharing joint attention;
- *participation* – supported participation, synchronised routines, sharing, turn-taking, making anticipatory movements;
- *involvement* – active participation, reaching out, joining in, commenting, making alternate exchanges, initiating changes;
- *achievement* – gaining, consolidating, practising skills, knowledge, concepts, expressing feelings and ideas with understanding.

(Based on Brown 1996, and adopted by QCA 2001a, as a framework for recognising attainment)

Originality and value

An *original*, creative response by a child with autism may occur within an individual activity or a group activity. It will need to be evaluated according to the extent to which the child has been supported (prompted) by others, and whether it took place in a structured or a free-play, spontaneous context. First and foremost, 'originality' has to be viewed in relation to a child's previous attainments – the extent to which a response reflects a new connection or combination of ideas specific to that particular child. Additionally, 'originality' then may be viewed not just in relation to other achievements by children with autism or even the wider disabled community, but also inclusively: as a contribution within the field of (for example) a particular art form.

Finally, in order for a response to be considered truly creative, the NACCCE (DfEE 1999) maintain that it has to be evaluated relative to the purpose: the *value* of an activity therefore, will vary according to the task in hand – after all, an original idea may be totally bizarre or faulty. Creative activity involves playing around with ideas and possibilities, some of which may be successful, others refashioned, rejected; it entails critical thinking and judgements along the way (in process) and afterwards (the outcome or product). Children with autism will need to be put in touch explicitly with an experience at each stage, to enable them to make connections and to reinforce their sense of themselves involved in the activity, and their ability to be proactive in relation to a purpose or goal.

Evaluating an experience may be individual or shared, with opinions possibly differing between the creator and others (teacher, peers, visitors). Children with autism may be challenged in acknowledging the perceptions of others, due to difficulty with 'theory of mind' (Baron-Cohen 1993). They will need to be supported in managing this interaction between generative and evaluative thinking, and the extent to which their responses may be judged to be (for example) effective, useful, enjoyable, valid or tenable, according to the particular activity in question (DfEE 1999).

The Calouste Gulbenkian Foundation (1982) identifies the value of creative and imaginative experiences, for giving the opportunity to:

- develop the full range of human potential;
- improve our capacity for thought, action and communication;
- nurture our feelings and sensibilities;
- extend our physical and perceptual skills;
- explore values;
- understand our own and other cultures.

'Creativity' is commonly associated with the arts, but is actually fundamental to advances in all areas of life (DfEE 1999). Creativity is recognised as an important aspect within a multi-dimensional view of intelligence (Eyre 1997), the component that can differentiate between those who do well and those who do brilliantly – a key indicator of giftedness, even. By the same token, 'creativity' would seem to be a critical element for enabling children with autism to aspire to a level of competence. This book argues that creative potential within everyone *can* be developed – and taught – through structured 'play' opportunities, both individually and in inclusive contexts. Through play-drama intervention it seeks to present a

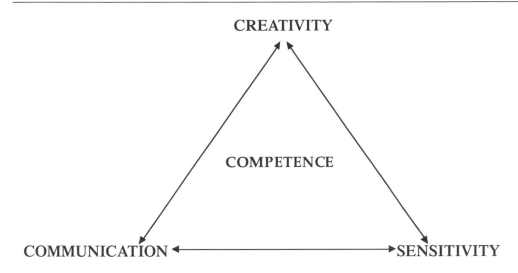

Figure 1.3 A 'triad of competence'

means to replace a 'triad of impairments' (Wing 1996) with a 'triad of competence': the development of more creative, flexible thinking, with associated gains in communication and greater sensitivity in social interaction (see Figure 1.3).

Playfulness and motivation

Monks' (1992) model of giftedness acknowledges that a child's potential (latent ability) will only be fully unleashed if two other variables are also present. The first of these is the opportunity to be creative within the particular activity, as indicated earlier. The second variable is actually the child's attitude to the activity itself – task commitment. The contention presented here, is that Monks' (1992) model is relevant for children of *all* abilities, and that *any* child will not achieve his or her potential within an activity if simply not motivated by it.

Certainly, play-based approaches have been used very successfully with children with autism (for example, the Options Approach – Kaufman 1976, 1994; Sherborne Movement – Sherborne 1990; Intensive Interaction – Nind and Hewett 1994; Sherratt 1999). Similarly, children with autism are often stimulated by arts experiences ('playful' in character), and many professionals comment that it is during arts activities that they seem to be most engaged and able to make the most meaningful contact. The difficulty, however, for professionals in all essentially 'playful' activities, is the extent to which they should become involved and risk 'intruding' into the experience: will this stifle the children's creativity? Should they nevertheless be made aware of new possibilities – and if so, at what point should the professional intervene? Will the activity then become hijacked and over-directive?

In play-drama intervention, it is crucially important that teachers offer experiences with clear boundaries within which to create, in order to prevent loss of physical or emotional control, or loss of control of ideas (Prokofiev 1994). Children with autism may also become very stressed if an activity seems vague and unfocused, or if the teacher seems insecure over its purpose. The 'feel good' motivational quality commonly experienced by participants in play and drama activity may be attributable to the deployment and respect for certain *empowerment* principles derived from therapy:

1. *patience* – allowing time for the child to respond: change and development are possible, but may take time; ensuring activities are planned initially for a child's present stage of development, with time to explore; not being tempted to force the pace;

2. *trust* – developing a relationship, 'being there' – attentive, as well as a reliable physical presence; keeping certain aspects of an activity the same, predictable from session to session;

3. *space* – respecting preferred places, and tolerance of physical proximity to others;

4. *containment and safety to explore* – making boundaries clear within which to explore, experiment and create, to support the release of feelings and acceptable responses and behaviour;

5. *dynamic of doing and being* – not overwhelming with a need to be constantly active: creative leaps may happen in moments of engaged stillness and reflection;

6. *developing a shared language* – establishing a foundation for communication, verbally and non-verbally, and investing meaning in spontaneous utterances and responses as an intention to communicate;

7. *timing* – sensitivity especially over when and how to give attention, to intervene or to introduce change; providing a balance of opportunities to transfer, consolidate and generalise learning through familiar, repeated activities, as well as new challenges, at the very least to prevent perseveration and over-reliance on obsessive favourite activities. (Based on Chesner 1995.)

As with other *interactive* methods (Collis and Lacey 1996; Peter 1998), the quality of the teacher–pupil relationship in play-drama interevention is crucial. The development of social interaction and communication will be dependent on a positive ethos based on negotiation, cooperation and an emphasis on diversity and individuality. This entails a sideways shift from more formal, directive approaches with children with autism, towards child-led initiatives and a genuine respect and responsiveness to a child's interests and needs – obsessions may be a useful starting point! While the teacher may have a covert agenda, the child should genuinely perceive his or her ultimate 'ownership' of the session: although the consequences of an activity may be anticipated (by the teacher), the teacher requires an open mind-set, and there should always be the element of surprise in the final outcome.

In both play and drama activities, the teacher should be there to facilitate understanding, and help children to think through and resolve any problems. Even though children with autism may not respond to praise as their mainstream peers, it is still important that approval should be given for their effort, not just a successful outcome. A bland 'good' or 'well done' may not be sufficient: children with autism will require a little more to be said, in order to explain what is deemed to be 'good' – for example, adding 'you have let me help you build a really high tower with those bricks'. Careful management of an activity should prevent 'failure' as such, but if it does arise, then teachers should ensure that the child with autism perceives this as an aspect of the activity, not of himself or herself.

The teacher may support children with autism also in incidentally reinforcing their sense of self, through involving them in meaningful evaluation in a way that will develop their *metacognition* – their awareness of themselves as thinking agents. For example, use of video and photographs of children with autism taken during a session may prompt recall of their involvement; in this way, they may learn to be proactive in making decisions based on their knowledge, understanding and growing heightened sense of resourcefulness.

Deci and Ryan (1985) claim that self-determination alongside competence is a fundamental human need, and that children will lose interest if they perceive their actions to be controlled by others. Children should be enabled to make choices confidently within secure boundaries, with the teacher clarifying to the child acceptable methods and short-term goals – the point of the activity otherwise may remain meaningless to the child with autism, who will experience difficulties in identifying an implicit purpose. Children with autism may feel more liberated in experiences where there is often not a 'right or wrong' answer, provided boundaries are gradually broadened and choices carefully paced to preserve their sense of security and allay anxieties over loss of control; in this way, through play-drama intervention they may gradually develop a more creative approach to problem-solving.

Play and drama: an integrating approach for autism

Play and drama share a narrative basis. Narrative is also the fabric of our understanding of the world: it is how we recognise that there are patterns and sequences in life. This is particularly true in understanding other people. Research has indicated the importance of make-believe play and narrative for children's eventual social competence. Play and drama can be effective tools for structuring children's development in learning to make-believe and understand narrative in social contexts. The particular power of drama-in-education is that it focuses explicitly on these social aspects of life.

Play and drama are rarely used with children with autism in any purposeful way. It could be argued that their 'triad of impairments' (Wing 1996) might seriously hinder children with autism from participating meaningfully in play and drama experiences: not only do they have difficulties with communication and social interaction to greater or lesser degrees, but also, by definition, their tendency towards rigidity of thought would appear fundamentally to militate against the kind of creativity and imagination that characterises play and drama activity. This is the nub of the difficulty – yet also the potential – for children with autism engaging purposefully in play and drama.

Play activity may provide structures within which to create, and at the same time 'fire up' the participants in emotionally charged contexts, thus *integrating* their cognitive strengths and essential 'playfulness' (see Figure 1.4). The developmental approach in play-drama intervention offers clear structures within which the latent ability of children with autism may be unleashed, with boundaries gradually being widened as children gain control of and confidence in their creative potential (Peter 2000b). Play-drama intervention may also make a crucial contribution towards redressing the fundamental impairment in *affective* functioning experienced by children with autism, and their consequent difficulties in evaluating meaning and seeing significance in situations.

A structured approach to developing play and extending children's make-believe in drama can make explicit how meanings may be constructed, and enable children with autism to make links with meanings in the real world (Peter 2000b). Drama has the explicit intention of exploring the implications of feeling responses, and to take make-believe play at the heart of the drama process into areas of learning. This may appeal to the logical, *cognitive* strengths of children with autism (Schopler and Olley 1982). Attitudes and opportunities for play and drama provided by school, home, peers and the wider community will all have a bearing on the extent to which the child with autism may flourish.

The popular idea that play is somehow 'light relief' from 'real work' is actually two-edged. While it is true that play may be an opportunity for more open-ended activity, teachers nevertheless require a secure (if covert) sense of direction and understanding of development. Paradoxically, this will actually enable them to respond more flexibly to individual children's initiatives, towards achieving their latent creative potential. Play-drama intervention provides secure frameworks within which children with autism may confidently learn to take initiative and make choices, and see them acted upon by others; changes may be gradually introduced, accepted and embraced.

Play-drama intervention may offer a powerful contribution to the development of *all* children's self-advocacy, as they learn how they can influence other people in different ways. For children with autism, play and drama also promote a thinking style that they tend to lack, and which can be modified through active engagement in such experiences. While containing distinct cognitive dimensions, play and drama activities are appealing simply because of their inherent playfulness. Teachers need to strive to retain the essence of this 'playfulness' and promote

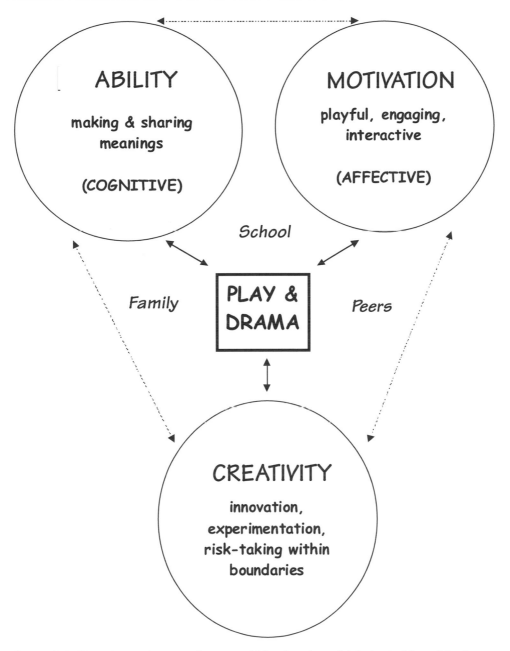

Figure 1.4 Play-drama intervention: a multi-factional model (adapted from Monks 1992)

creativity at every opportunity. Play and drama are integrating and *dynamic*: they entail ongoing interaction between the actual *process* and (at times) the *product* from the experience. It is no coincidence that in drama, the term 'play' refers to both the activity and the outcome!

So, why play? Why not?

CHAPTER 2

Play and Children with Autism

This chapter aims to probe more deeply into the play behaviour of children with autism, and explain the value of developing their potential for make-believe and narrative understanding through play-drama intervention. It is through teachers' understanding of the difficulties that face children with autism in their play, that effective intervention strategies may be designed that will underpin the development of their potential social competence. These difficulties will be described, and illustrated with practical examples from across the autistic spectrum.

The autistic way of thinking and playing

Children with autism are often relatively skilled in areas such as visuo-spatial tasks (for example, completing jigsaw puzzles), and seem to use rational thinking processes more effectively than 'free-flow' processes (Bruner 1986; Bruce 1991). A child with autism may show a remarkable *logical* ability in recognising the behaviours of others through interpreting these in terms of behaviour that they have previously experienced. Yet the same child may have considerable difficulty in predicting the future actions of the same person. It is plausible that this lack of *empathetic* understanding is due to a problem in juxtaposing the rational and free-flow thought processes (Harris 2000).

In order to construct a coherent understanding, it is necessary to bring together the observable and the *possible*, the conscious and the *sub-conscious*, the rational and the *emotional* (Damasio 1999). For children with autism, an inability or tendency not to bring these mental entities together results in difficulties with building complex concepts such as planning, sequencing, and understanding the self and others. The consequences of autistic brain functioning also result in limited play behaviour: when given play materials or equipment they rarely use these to play in a creative and imaginative way – most children with autism occupy themselves with the physical characteristics of the items. This frequently results in the items being disregarded after a brief inspection to see, for example, what is under that flap or whether dolly's arm can be turned all the way round.

Jarrold *et al.* (1996: 227) explain the lack of spontaneity in the symbolic play of children with autism as the result of impairment in 'generating the retrieval strategies necessary for bringing pretend schemas into use'. In other words, although children with autism are capable of symbolising in pretence, they have difficulty in generating the necessary mental processes to use the imaginative image. It is not surprising that children who have difficulties in switching between rational and free-flow modes of thought would have difficulty in spontaneously using pretence. The conscious mind cannot easily switch from a rational, real-life 'window' to an alternative world of pretence.

Most children with autism do not develop spontaneous symbolic play, yet when *prompted* to play, those that have symbolic capacity in their language may begin to use symbolic acts with play materials (Lewis and Boucher 1988; Jarrold *et al.* 1993, 1996; Charman and Baron-Cohen 1997). For example, when asked 'what can you do with these?' certain children are able to put materials together as if they are something else, so that an empty cardboard box may become a garage for a toy car, or a bowl for dolly's soup. In a prompted situation, the child does not have to generate the retrieval of this image and is led into producing it: something triggers a switch to the imaginary world. Children with autism may then be enabled to understand and use pretence, which challenges the notion that children with autism are 'not able to play'.

Prompts for play for children with autism may be external or internal. External prompts can involve an adult giving explicit instruction, or perhaps drawing attention to another child playing with something in the corner of the room. An internal prompt involves a thought triggering the switch to the pretence 'window'. This could be through an associated or random mental image coming into the conscious mind; it could also be through association with a strong positive emotional image. It is probable that prompts that involve positive affective experience of previous pretend play events would trigger a switch into pretence. In other words, a strong emotional memory associated with a particular make-believe experience would create a desire to become involved in play once more.

However, the elicitation of such responses in children with autism is a long way from the absorbing spontaneous play that is frequently seen in normally developing children. Libby *et al.* (1998) found that the *symbolic play* acts of children with autism were limited almost entirely to object substitutions (one object standing for another). The *role-play* of children with autism is often stereotypical and tends not to involve attributing a mental state to inanimate objects (for example, 'my dolly is hungry'). When entering into role-play, a child follows and improvises upon the flexible narrative of another – often the words are not scripted and the child must take on some of the surface characteristics to signify that the role has been taken; these characteristics are incorporated into the child's own understanding of the world (Harris 2000). It follows, that the relative lack of role-play in children with autism contributes to their later difficulty in understanding the minds of others.

Play and the autistic 'triad of impairments'

The thought processes responsible for creative representations in symbolic pretend play are similar to those involved in social understanding, the social use of language and some aspects of semantic language that require highly fluid understanding of changing meanings. Children with autism experience difficulties in communication, social interaction and flexible thinking. It is clear that without intervention, this 'triad of impairments' (Wing 1996) will severely undermine their ability to engage in pretend play with others, and hamper their development of empathy.

Play and difficulties in social interaction

One of the authors involved a group of children with autism in play with puppets and a large cardboard box that had been adapted to look like a television set. They were told that they could use the puppets to act out a story like a show on the television for the rest of the class who would be the viewers. The remaining children were asked to sit around the television in a semi-circle and wait for the show to start. The play episodes were completed and enjoyed by each player, even though the quality of the play was variable. While sounds of giggles and squeals of delight could frequently be heard coming from the box, the children appeared to have little desire or intention to perform or share this excitement with others. Nevertheless, all the children appeared to be aware of the attention of the other children, and would increase their efforts if they heard the audience laughing at the antics of the puppets.

Despite this, one common feature was shared among all the players: all the children with autism failed to communicate their pretence to the people watching. They either did not speak at all, or else mumbled towards the puppets. The children did not put on a 'performance', and often found no reason to face the audience. They would continue to play with their back turned, or else under the table where no one could see. The children lacked the social understanding to communicate their play to the other children. To redeem their capacity for meaningful communication to an audience, they would need to acquire an understanding of their ability to influence others that goes beyond a simple cause-effect response to an antic. They would have to gain a consolidated understanding of the connection between their own mental states and consequent behaviour, and that other people possess similar mental states that are affected by external stimuli.

However, this play episode indicates the latent ability of those children with autism to engage in play with a clear structure, the appealing props providing visual hooks and the necessary motivation. It also suggests that those children might have some of the underlying predisposition and necessary apparatus for engaging in social play.

Children with autism often experience fundamental difficulties in engaging with others and implicitly understanding that other people share a joint focus of interest. One boy, Hamish, rarely made eye contact, although he was not averse to it. Each morning he would bring a toy from home into school, and would often take it out of his pocket during the course of the day. Unlike most of the other children in his class, Hamish would not show the toy to anyone else or say 'look what I've got!' Instead, he would create ritualised sequences with the toy that others were not invited to join. When other children huddled in a corner of the room, he rarely investigated to find out what was happening to interest the other children. Hamish was interested in the computer, watching videos of action heroes and jumping, running and climbing. All of these he would perform as solitary pursuits. The play of other children was generally meaningless and valueless to him.

For something to be meaningful, it has to connect the emotions and cognition, creating an attitude towards the event. The event must invoke an experience of (for example) excitement, pleasure, surprise, anger, etc. The child must also be able to assess the event easily, using his or her understanding of similar previous events. The connection between the emotional and cognitive systems brings the child's senses and mind into a single focus, and by so doing, makes a link between the self and the outside world. A meaningful event often creates a moment of intense engagement and anticipation, of mild uncertainty, of wondering 'will she do this or will she do that?' This tension, of course, is the cornerstone of play and drama – and of learning, as the child's thinking is challenged (akin to Piaget's concept of 'disequilibrium').

However, children with autism often do not engage in this way in normal social interactions and fail to engage with the countless opportunities that present themselves every day. They often fail to find meaning within ordinary interactions, whereas normally developing children are tuned in to look for these opportunities. For normally developing children, this ability develops in the early months of life, and forms the backbone of social learning. Even from a few hours old, babies are able to imitate expressions on the faces of their mother. However, the human face appears to hold little interest or salience for children with autism (Volkmar 1987), neither do they display the usual preference for maternal speech (Klin 1991, 1992). This relative disinterest and non-responsiveness will necessarily undermine early interaction between parents and their child with autism, which has been shown to be so important for subsequent development.

It is not clear whether children with autism lack a predisposition for social understanding, or whether they experience difficulty in the thinking processes that develop on these early foundations. *Joint attention* with others on a shared object of mutual interest is thought to be a necessary prerequisite for symbolic play (Leslie 1994). Research has also evidenced a strong relationship between affect, language and cognition, as found in joint attention experiences (Mundy 1995; Mundy and Crowson 1997; Bates *et al.* 1979). It is clear too, that in normally developing children, symbolic play is enhanced through collaborating with peers in social pretend play (Howes 1992). However, as indicated above, children with autism usually lack an awareness of the interest of others in their play.

Play and difficulties in communication

Gregory was a six-year-old boy with severe autism and challenging behaviour. He used very little speech: his vocalisations were mainly used for communicating his annoyance, for example, when people interfered with his routines, or when he was frustrated at having stacked his beakers incorrectly. Gregory was interested in creepy crawlies of various kinds, particularly beetles. His favourite playtime occupation was looking for beetles under stones and in damp places. When Gregory managed to find one, he would watch it scuttle away with an intensity and excitement that was rarely seen in other situations. Sometimes when this became too much, Gregory would catch the beetle, often resulting in him squashing it between his thumb and forefinger, or under the palm of his hand.

One day in the classroom, Gregory's teacher tried to move one of his stacking beakers into a position where he might find it before his tower collapsed. Through the corner of his eye, he saw movement and squashed her hand to the table. The teacher exclaimed 'Ow . . . beetle squashed . . . Oh dear!' Gregory smiled. The teacher made her hand into a crawling beetle shape and walked it across Gregory's desk. Gregory flattened it once more, but this time a little more gently. As she repeated this sequence, the teacher found that his squashing actions became more exaggerated and sometimes were accompanied by a grunting noise. By repeating this sequence, the teacher established a predictable pattern to the game.

The teacher was also able to extend this game and create opportunities for Gregory to develop his communication skill. Instead of repeating the game as Gregory expected, she paused. The beetle did not walk across the table. Gregory waited until he realised that something was wrong; he looked into her face and eyes. Interpreting this as a request, the teacher immediately awoke the beetle. Within a few more repeats of pausing for him, Gregory was consistently using eye-gaze as a means to request. Over the following days, the teacher introduced a series of plastic beetles and shiny homemade beetle puppets into the game, and started to move the game to other areas of the room. Eventually she introduced a modification of this game into the playground. Gregory shouted 'Go, beetle!' and a toy beetle was pulled in a jerky fashion for him to catch. This game became popular with several other children in the playground, and soon several children were joining Gregory to shout 'Go, beetle!'

In this example, Gregory increased his communication rate through having a reason to interact with others. This was a very positive use of social play, in which an existing interest was harnessed to create a means of finding pleasure in communication.

It follows that the communication difficulties experienced by children with autism in their play are closely related to impairments in social understanding. Even normally developing children with no speech will use pointing, eye gaze, gesture and manipulation to communicate their thoughts, because they perceive these as important – and important enough to share. Many children with autism do not develop effective communication through speech, sign language or using symbols, other than to make functional requests; for example, to ask for a drink. Even in more able children with autism, communication is often highly restricted or pedantic and formal.

Children with autism have particular difficulties also in the way that they use *non-verbal communication*. They are often impaired in the use of gesture and posture to communicate meaning. The absence or late development of pointing to indicate something of interest is particularly significant, as pointing often opens the floodgates to new communicative possibilities. As shown above, understanding the intentions of others is founded in early social interactions with parents and caregivers. These typically involve the meaningful use of eye-gaze to indicate an intention to introduce a change in behaviour. Teasing and tickling games are quickly understood by normally developing children in the first year of life; similarly, following the eye-gaze or point of another person.

However, research has provided evidence of how in play situations, the communication of children with autism can notably increase. Children with autism are often very poor at using eye-gaze in everyday life; however, in social games, they may use eye-gaze as much as their peers without autism (Whittaker 1996). Even those children who tend to use very low levels of communication have been observed to change the type of communication from mainly requests for food and protests, to requests for positive social interaction – the continuation of non-verbal social games such as tickling and rough and tumble (Potter and Whittaker 2001). Rough and tumble games are commonly played with children with autism (Nind and Hewett 1994); children who normally avoid eye-contact frequently do make sustained and meaningful eye-contact in these situations.

Play and inflexible thought processes

A four-year-old boy with autism, Daniel, enjoyed the story of 'Elmer the Patchwork Elephant' (McGee 1987). He enjoyed listening to the story being read by the teacher or watching it on video. The teacher bought a fabric toy Elmer, thinking that this would motivate Daniel to extend his interest into play. As the teacher turned the pages of the book, Daniel enjoyed seeing this colourful toy become animated. He particularly enjoyed seeing Elmer shout 'BOO!', and would fall about in paroxysms of laughter.

Subsequently, the teacher decided to modify the story so that Elmer played different tricks on the other creatures. As soon as there was a deviation from the familiar narrative, Daniel became highly agitated and tried to run away. He also refused to join in with this modified story on a further occasion, and would only listen to the story on video. Daniel was upset by the teacher's attempts to change the story because he had a very fixed idea about what a narrative should be doing: he thought that this story of Elmer was the story rather than a story of Elmer. Daniel had been thrown by the teacher's use of the storybook at the same time as she wished to modify the familiar narrative – the book acted as a visual structure that served to confuse him.

The teacher was able to make some progress with Daniel's restricted thought processes by working through play. She introduced a story in which some ordinary plain grey elephants were looking for Elmer. The elephants looked all round the classroom, under the chairs and behind the feet of any nearby children. Daniel was asked to hide Elmer under his chair, which of course was the last place that anyone would look. When the teacher's elephant found Elmer, there were hoots of laughter from all concerned. Daniel tolerated this at first, but soon grew to enjoy the game. He continued to develop his play by using a set of cards with different scenes shown on them, which could be placed on a filmstrip-style storyboard. Daniel was encouraged to choose the sequence of the cards and to animate the characters. Although he still had a very rigid play style there was some evidence of increasing flexibility. For example, Daniel would attempt to repeat the same sequence of play cards in order to re-enact a previously satisfying narrative. The teacher was able to extend Daniel's play by introducing attractive toys and materials at key moments in the narrative, so that the actions he used were modified in the light of these additions.

Children with autism experience an overwhelming tendency towards repetition in their actions and thought processes. They are impaired in the fluency with which they can spontaneously produce a range of responses from a single stimulus (Turner 1997, 1999). It is not clear whether children with autism lack this flexibility owing to difficulties in the generation or in the inhibition or monitoring of their thoughts and actions. Daniel may have been unable to generate play sequences and therefore was reliant on repeating a prescribed narrative. Or he may have been unable to inhibit the potency of the original story so that each time it was started, the sequence was too powerful to override with variations on the theme. It may have been that Daniel could not align the story, the actions of the toy and the adaptations to the story at the same time.

In order to perform these mental actions, Daniel would need to understand the gist of the story and be able to apply it to a shifting narrative. However, he did not look for the underlying meanings in the narrative (such as boredom, teasing, humour and novelty); instead, he remembered a sequence of words and elephant behaviours. The implication is that in order to prompt pretence in children with autism, teachers should be careful just to provide the necessary fragments of information as potential pivots, and not to present these within powerfully restrictive structures. This is an important key for unlocking the play potential of children with autism.

Play potential of children with autism

Hamish climbed onto a table and standing tall, bellowed and screamed for all he was worth. He hit himself repeatedly; his fists mostly fell around his chest and shoulders. Teachers in the classroom had not seen Hamish behave like this before. Although he was often non-compliant and insisted on doing things his way, he rarely used challenging behaviours and certainly not in this way. With a startled look of apprehension on his face, Hamish leaped from the table and rolled across the floor. Scrambling to his feet, Hamish threw himself against the classroom door and groaning, collapsed to the floor. To the amazement of everyone in the room, he ran back to the table and repeated the process. Unfortunately on the third repeat, the school caretaker opened the door. Hamish leaped from the table and ran at him with a look of glazed determination in his eyes. The resulting mass of bodies writhing on the floor was enough to ensure that Hamish was not allowed to continue with these behaviours.

Hamish only rarely played spontaneously. It was not until several days later that the school staff realised what Hamish had been doing in the above incident. He had been to the cinema and had been very impressed by a newly released and somewhat light-hearted adaptation of the Tarzan story. In this version of the film Tarzan swings through the jungle on leafy vines, but on one occasion miscalculates, and crashes headfirst into a large tree and groaning, slides to the ground. Had Hamish simply been re-enacting this in the classroom? The realisation that Hamish had been playing came as a surprise to the staff – and a begrudging relief to the caretaker!

What does this play episode tell us about Hamish and about the play potential of other children with autism?

Was Hamish using symbolic play?

For play to be considered *symbolic*, a child has to use at least one of the following transformations:

- object substitution – for example, a stick becomes a sword;
- attribution of false properties – for example, the sword is very sharp;
- imaginary appearance or reappearance – for example, duelling with a non-existent opponent.

The play of children with autism has been described as 'unsymbolic' (Leslie 1987). However, in the example above, Hamish developed his own variation of Tarzan swinging through the jungle. The adaptation that Hamish made to this narrative involved him in *imagining* a strong vine hanging down when nothing existed in reality. He also crashed into objects across the other side of the classroom – these were *substitutions* for trees in the jungle. By standing on a table initially, Hamish *represented* being off the ground, perhaps in another tree. Hamish also displayed expressions of pain as he writhed about on the floor. In this, he *attributed feelings* to his character, when he himself did not experience them. Hamish had used symbolic acts to represent the features of this narrative that were meaningful to him, and which were certainly not copied from the play behaviours of anyone else.

Alternatively, could Hamish's play be considered 'symbolically delayed' (Baron-Cohen 1989)? This could be judged in relation to *language ability*. Levels of pretend play tend to show a high correlation with language use and comprehension, as both rely on the production and manipulation of symbols (Cicchetti *et al.* 1994). Hamish had been assessed at the age of five years, as having an understanding of speech at a level comparable with most normally developing children of 24 months (Reynell Developmental Language Scales 1977). A normally developing child of that age might be expected to use simple sequences that involve single acts of pretence. However, Hamish linked at least three symbolic acts, which would imply that he could play at a level at least comparable with his language ability.

Was Hamish spontaneous in his play?

In the above example, Hamish had *not* been taking part in a structured activity in which play actions were deliberately elicited. He had not been asked to replicate the film that he had previously seen – he had not been asked to play at all. What then, had prompted this play episode? Usually Hamish did not play spontaneously: given a box of plastic animals, he would quickly dismiss them as meaningless; asked to cook dinner in the playhouse, he would snort in disgust and run the other way. Although Hamish was unable to communicate what had prompted his play on this occasion, it is possible to identify some precipitating features.

Although no contemporaneous prompt had been given, Hamish was seemingly intrigued by the idea of Tarzan swinging through the jungle and crashing into the trees. This clearly had some *emotional resonance* for him: Hamish was a boisterous child who loved rough and tumble and watching things crashing, whether toy cars or children in the playground. The crashing sequence in the Tarzan film must have been highly meaningful to him, and produced an affective response that prompted him to jump off the table. Yet there was also a *narrative structure* in place that allowed Hamish to sequence the actions, based on the storyline in the Tarzan film. This was then reconstructed in a way that was meaningful to him.

It is probable that Hamish reconstructed this narrative as it was enacted, rather than planning it in advance: as he stood on the table shouting and waving his arms, the narrative prompted him to find a way of doing what he wanted to do next, for example, swing through the trees. Similarly, when the school caretaker walked in through the door and instantly became a part of the sequence, Hamish modified his reconstructed narrative. Thus the familiar storyline offered him a structure, and the crashing action provided an affective prompt. As this was meaningful to him, he became inspired to play, even though in most other situations he was distinctly uninspired to play.

Harris and Levers (2000) suggest that play in children with autism is *restricted* because the children are impaired in the generation or execution of internal plans or narratives. Yet despite his autism, Hamish was able to take the storyline from the Tarzan film and develop his own narrative from it; he was able also to modify the narrative that he had created to accommodate the appearance of the caretaker. Hamish had demonstrated a particular *spontaneous* quality to his play hitherto unseen, and this clearly revealed his *play potential*.

Enabling pretence in children with autism

Research has shown that it is possible to shape the emergence of pretend play in children with autism, through systematically rewarding desired symbolic play acts. For example, direct reinforcement of desired symbolic play acts through associated play activities has proved effective in teaching children with autism to engage in make-believe at a level comparable to their normally developing language-matched peers (Stahmer and Stahmer 1995). Thorp *et al.* (1995) similarly used this approach to teach more advanced *sociodramatic play* to children with autism, with the adult reinforcing the child's initiatives in the emerging narrative with relevant equipment associated with the development in the script. The children made progress both in their play and in some language and social skills, and demonstrated key characteristics of sociodramatic play; for example:

- *role playing* – pretending to cook dinner;
- *object substitution* – pretending that a wooden block was an ingredient for dinner;
- *social interaction* – pretending to go shopping with someone else;
- *verbal communication* – asking someone what they would like to eat;
- *persistence* (maintaining a narrative from beginning to end, with at least four consecutive elements) e.g. pretending to drive to the shops, buying food, paying for the food and driving home again.

It appears that there is a positive relationship between language skills and levels of prompted pretend play in children with autism. The thought processes responsible for creative representations in symbolic pretend play are similar to those involved in social understanding, the social use of language and some aspects of semantic language that require highly fluid understanding of changing meanings. Similarly, the level of symbolic play in children with autism is significantly higher in prompted play, and at a level comparable with their chronologically normally developing peers – provided that the adult times intervention at an appropriate moment.

Under such 'scaffolded' conditions, children with autism show reduced obsessive and repetitive behaviour, because they are assisted with their difficulty in retrieving new thoughts and actions (Turner 1997). Clear play structures are more likely to enable children with autism to access new thoughts and actions associated with the particular play activity. It could be argued that using such structure causes children with autism to become reliant on the same cues being present, or presented, in order to remember or respond. Although the research studies above used approaches that were script-led and highly structured, the children did not restrict their play to the contexts and cues involved in the intervention programmes, and they used play skills in other situations and with other people.

However, it is possible for children with autism to be enabled to engage in make-believe at a level that actually goes *beyond training* them to respond to play cues or re-enact play sequences. The combination of meaningful, enjoyable play contexts together with structure is the crucial catalyst for facilitating spontaneous pretend play: a means of assisting the child with autism towards a better *understanding* of role taking and the development of empathy. Beyer and Gammeltoft (2000) advocate using a clearly demarcated play space and carefully selected motivating toys, as well as establishing an emotional bond with children with autism, in order to engage them in increasingly complex play sequences. These two elements – an *enabling structure* and *meaningful experience* – are also evident in the above examples, and in each case contributed to the realisation of the play potential of the particular children concerned:

Gregory: his play was structured by the teacher *scaffolding* – building on one of his behaviours – and then extending the sequence one step at a time; he was motivated because the beetle theme gave him an interest in the actions of the teacher, who very carefully monitored Gregory's continuing interest in the play at each change that she introduced.

Daniel: the story of Elmer provided him with a structure, but this proved too strong: weakening the familiar narrative, while retaining some of its *motivating elements*, enabled him to engage more flexibly.

Hamish: the *storyline* of the Tarzan film provided a structure, aspects of which were brought back to mind and gave him clear guidance about what to do next as the ape-man; he was motivated to play because the behaviour of the Tarzan character had a boisterous appeal, being much like his own behaviour.

In order for children with autism to develop symbolic play, it appears necessary to prompt them in some way. However, using a clear structure may *reduce* the need for prompting in time, as they learn to use internally generated pretend play. Sherratt (2002) describes a three-phase structured intervention programme to teach children with autism to use symbolic play, including use of highly affective techniques (exaggerated, melodramatic expressions and reactions by the teacher). Each phase lasted approximately five weeks, and comprised play sessions of about forty minutes:

- *Phase 1* – play sequences based on familiar stories are provided, with the teacher modelling possible simple symbolic transformations; for example, a box to be a porridge bowl for each of the bears in the story of Goldilocks.
- *Phase 2* – more flexible play sequences with structure provided through a prescribed range of equipment, and the teacher demonstrating multiple transformations; for example, the teacher selects from a range of footwear, and exclaims, 'Now I have my Wellingtons on, I can splash in a puddle – oops! I've slipped over . . .'
- *Phase 3* – the teacher provides structure through a versatile range of equipment including found sources (boxes, lengths of cloth), but does not model or prompt a particular play response.

At the end of the programme, many of the children demonstrated novel and *spontaneous* symbolic play, including attributing false properties to objects and imaginary themes. While an implicit structure was provided in all the research studies cited above, in the work of Sherratt (2002) the structures involved were *explicit*. It is notable too, that the children involved made particularly rapid progress, with some evidence of actual creativity in their play. Why should this be so?

Play and drama: an intervention for autism

Why should play have such potency for children like Hamish? Why could developing pretence enable children with autism to learn more effectively? Although there is insufficient evidence to state categorically which processes and mechanisms are involved, two systems may be important. One of these involves the *brain and chemical processes* that may trigger and moderate pretence, so that children are enabled to use their imagination. The second involves a *psychological process* in which they learn to create and share meanings within make-believe narrative frameworks. Both of these systems have substantial potential for a wider understanding of the social world and the developing social competence of children with autism.

Brain activity during imaginative play

For the child to invoke pretence it is necessary to adopt a mental position in which reality is put to one side and an 'as if' world is explored. This attitude is produced using a complex series of neural and chemical processes interconnecting with brain structures. It is likely that these involve core parts of the brain that are responsible for representing emotional experience. Pathways from this core or mid-brain allow the speedy transmission of chemicals that enable the mind to 'slip out of gear' and enter a world of pretence. It is probable that the chemical Acetylcholine (ACh) is most closely associated with this process. ACh is commonly linked with other mental states that involve free-flow thinking, and which have similarities with pretence and play; for example, daydreaming, hallucinations, quiet reflection, creative problem solving, dreaming and sleep.

Acetylcholine has an important function in switching on free-association thinking processes. Dreams, for example, are often associated with visual images that are mixed and matched in a way that would not normally be accepted by the fully conscious mind. In a dreaming state, the levels of ACh are relatively high: the brain reduces its activity in the outer brain and increases the activity of the inner brain (Hobson and Stickgold 1994). ACh thus creates the conditions for free associations in dreaming. It follows that this same flexibility may be generated through stimulating the production of ACh in play. This is significant for children with autism in targeting an aspect of brain activity that is known to be under-functioning, and which otherwise may result in their tendency towards rigidity of thought.

The release of Acetylcholine triggers a loosely associated network of mental images and facilitates the adoption of an imaginary, 'as if' world; it also energises the connections that enable greater free-association thinking. The repeated use of these brain structures will strengthen the connections between all these sites of mental activity. In other words, the more the child plays, the more his or her capacity for creative thinking will be increased; the child will also be better placed to engage in spontaneous play. The implication is that the more children with autism use pretence, the better they will become at generating it, and the more they will be disposed to engage in it spontaneously. Figure 2.1 illustrates a possible neural mechanism that is involved in pretence. Points A, B, C and D refer to possible key points for intervention (to be explained more fully later): capturing the child's attention, ensuring their emotional engagement, moderating language, and ensuring an appropriate structure.

In normally developing children, play is inherently pleasurable, and the *affective* experiences associated with it become linked to representations of play behaviours in the mind. It is probable that those areas of the brain responsible for representing feelings and connecting these appropriately (evaluation of meaning) are also under-

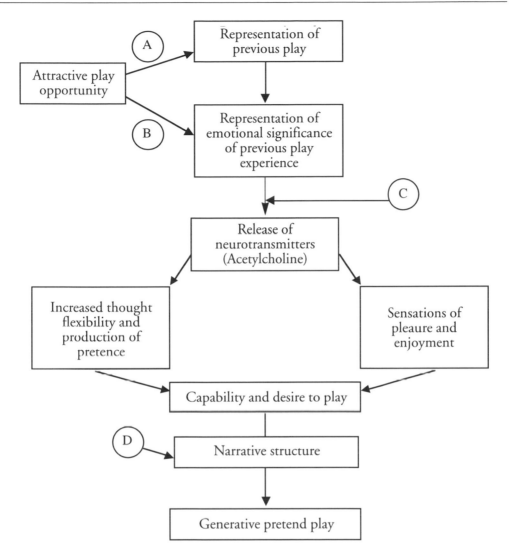

Figure 2.1 Neural processes in play

functioning in children with autism. This may explain why children with autism are capable of the representational processes necessary in pretence, but do not generate this pretence spontaneously. What may be lacking is an appreciation of the *emotional potential* – the intrinsic reward – of a play experience. This emotional resonance is also crucial for developing a coherent view of the world.

As stated earlier, in order to develop a cohesive conceptualisation of the world, a child needs to integrate the recognition of related mental representations with an associated affective (emotional) significance or personal meaning ('I like this', 'that upsets me', 'a chair is good for sitting on', etc.). It is the affective representations that create the conditions for *coherence* to take place. Events that have a personal meaning become connected by a thread – a thread that is a conceptualisation of self. This thread enables the mind to draw together associated meaningful representations. In a state of pretence, the brain is enabled to scan over a much wider range of possible associations and meaningful patterns.

However, unless affective brain activity is stimulated in children with autism, and unless experiences acquire an emotional resonance, their view of the world will remain fragmentary and they will remain isolated. Approaches to intervention that appeal primarily to the logical cognitive strengths of children with autism will be imbalanced, and result in skewed development based on the misplaced notion of incontrovertible 'impairment'. In contrast, an approach based on play can target that affective aspect of brain functioning in children with autism, and connect emotional responses to their actions. This may directly shore up the impaired 'sense of self' that is at the core of their difficulties, and facilitate a more coherent view of the world.

Playing purposefully

When normally developing children engage in purposeful play, three inter-related processes occur almost simultaneously (see Figure 2.2). A child will instantaneously integrate perceptual recognition of (for example) a toy car, and associated feelings ('I like that') with sequences of actions ('I can push the car into the garage and fill it up with petrol'). This feeling response to a stimulus links with the perceptual representation (here the symbolic representation of a car) and an awareness of possibilities within a narrative framework (here, the key events in a trip to a petrol station). The crucial trigger in generating purposeful play is the emotional association with a cue or stimulus, based on the memory of a previous experience. This affective memory will motivate – prompt – the child into action through a desire to replicate it.

A *structured* approach that has play at its core will enable the teacher to pace development in the three inter-related processes that will address the fundamental impairments in children with autism. The structure of the play experience will provide sequences of pivotal moments where the child may learn to make increasingly complex choices and decisions. In this way, play experiences may become gradually more challenging, and the 'narrative framework' extended. As children are put on their mettle in play, so will such experiences acquire an emotional resonance for them, and be perceived as opportunities for meaningful engagement – having something in it 'for them'. Developing this awareness through play experiences with others will also enable them to discover intrinsic pleasure in relating to other people.

Children with autism need to learn to recognise play behaviour and to associate it with this three-way internalised representational network; this may be the key to

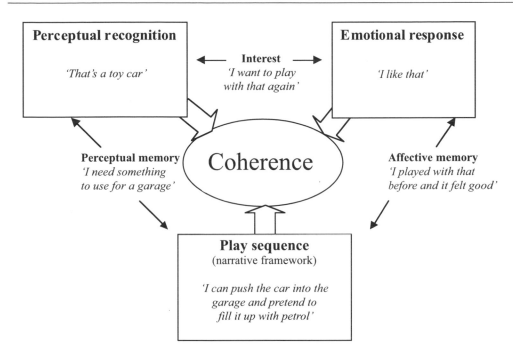

Figure 2.2 Purposeful play

unlocking spontaneous, purposeful play. The implication for the teacher is a responsibility to ensure that play experiences are *meaningful*, so that the child will generate the associated feeling responses. In social play contexts, the teacher has the opportunity to infuse the play activity with emotional resonance, and actively scaffold the creation of a shared meaning with the child. (For example, mirroring a child's spontaneous reaction to a development in the play activity and reinforcing the emotional significance to the child.) Teaching children with autism to perceive play behaviours is important if they are to prioritise these among the myriad actions that children use. In order to achieve this, the child must recognise the actions of others as relating to play and not to the real world. Figure 2.1 indicates possible points of intervention by the teacher in play activity:

(A) When the teacher introduces new play (or drama) opportunities, the child with autism needs to perceive the behaviour used as signifying play. The clear use of play markers will demonstrate that a mental stance of pretence or play has been taken, and will trigger the necessary neural processes that facilitate purposeful play. For example, exaggerated voice intonation and rhythmic patterns to speech, overstated gestures and facial expressions, and inflated expressions of affect towards another person or object (Potter and Whittaker 2001; Sherratt 1999, 2002; Peter 1994).

(B) Initially, the process of perception building will require adults to make play and social behaviours appear highly pleasurable and larger than life. It is important that children with autism develop feelings of excitement, joy and satisfaction that are associated with acts of pretence and the pretence of others. The role of the teacher is to facilitate an excitement in the play if this not spontaneous.

(C) The teacher should ensure that language and object prompts are not too dominant so that they block thought flexibility. The use of too much language or using object prompts that are too suggestive of previous behavioural patterns should be avoided, to allow the child to use free-flow thought.

(D) The teacher also needs to ensure that there is a sufficient narrative structure to enable the child to embed the play and extend it by linking associated, relevant and meaningful ideas. It is also necessary to provide a structure that is just sufficient – not so potent that it restricts play.

Unless possibilities are presented to children with autism, their play is at risk of becoming stuck, resulting in characteristic repetitive behaviour, such as obsessive twiddling of string. While this may have emotional resonance for the child, it will lack the learning potential to extend and develop understanding. Learning how to play purposefully necessarily involves linking meaningful actions within a sequence; in other words, discovering and exploring the effect and consequences of key moments. This can be regarded essentially as a 'narrative': a framework within which meanings are encapsulated within key moments that impel a course of action. Play experiences can be solitary; for example, stacking and then knocking down nesting beakers will reinforce understanding of the relationship of objects in space. However, if social understanding is to be developed, children also need to be able to harness culturally defined symbols and representations within a shared narrative framework.

Pretence: the route to social competence!

The route to developing social understanding – and growing social competence – lies in enabling children with autism to engage in pretence with others, where social meanings may be generated and explored. For children to engage in make-believe, they need to develop their *symbolic understanding*, in order to perceive the cultural significance of words (spoken or written), visual images and icons and metaphors. Secondly, they need to understand and *use representations with others* in the creation of shared meanings; in other words, be able to participate in a shared narrative. An intervention programme needs to embrace both these strands, so that children with autism may learn explicitly how representations and shared meanings may be created.

It is also crucially important that a structured approach to play with children with autism is developed in social contexts from the outset. For example, Wolfberg (1999) has shown the value of inclusive play groupings for such children. *Social play* will open up learning opportunities in collaborative situations, showing how shared meanings may be created within increasingly complex play structures (narrative frameworks). Initially this may be through replicating early caregiver–child interactive games and 'joint action formats' (Bruner 1975b), involving shared attention on an object of interest. This may then develop into functional play that involves relating objects in predictable play sequences, and explicit teaching of representational use of objects and pretend actions. As their understanding of symbolism becomes consolidated, so children with autism may learn to engage more purposefully in make-believe with others and with more regard for the feelings and intentions of others.

Introducing strategies from *drama-in-education* offers children with autism a reflective window: it will enable them to explore shared meanings embedded in make-believe, and to understand better how social meanings are constructed. Drama-in-education enables children to understand social narratives – how it is that actions, events become linked as a result of human behaviour – and explore implications of their own mental states and those of others. They may also learn how to manipulate the theatre form (the art form of drama) both within analogous contexts in the make-believe and in real life. In this way, they may learn how to influence other people and be instrumental in creating social narratives – and with growing social competence.

A structured approach to play and drama will enable children with autism to learn through – and benefit from – processes like those observed in their normally developing peers. Play-drama intervention is founded on the conviction that many children with autism have an underlying potential that is based upon latent abilities and predispositions, and that these can be harnessed, coaxed and developed through meaningful social experiences. It is apparent that an overtly structured, developmental approach can teach children with autism to develop pretend play and enable them to use this spontaneously in free play situations. In this way, they may gradually learn to understand the roles that other people take, and how to simulate the thoughts and actions of others; this will enable a better understanding of other people. Play-drama intervention brings a notion of social competence rather than 'impairment' within the grasp of many children.

CHAPTER 3

Learning to Play

From previous chapters, it is apparent that in play-drama intervention strategies need to be made explicit to children with autism. They will not spontaneously learn to play in the same way as their normally developing peers. This chapter explores the teacher's role in developing play in children with autism, and provides a framework for leading them towards imaginative play and narrative understanding. These are essential, not only as components of make-believe (the bed-rock of children's eventual social competence), but also for promoting creative, flexible thinking.

Assessment is critical to good teaching and forms the basis of intervention in play. In particular, techniques are described to assess the play *capability* of children with autism, with illustrations of how this information can be used to make judgements about teaching strategies. A series of play structures is presented, each designed to promote development from repetitive and narrow play towards more flexible, spontaneous and imaginative play. Finally, a summary is provided of classroom management issues, together with specific pointers regarding teaching play to children with autism. (Useful practical resources for play are listed in Appendix D.)

The reader's attention is also drawn to Appendices A and B, which support this chapter. In Appendix A, a number of practical examples are provided of teaching strategies and possible techniques for children at different stages of play development. It is intended that these will act as a stimulus to applying the approach advised in this chapter, rather than being a list of prescribed activities. In Appendix B, techniques are described for teaching social play to children with autism, which needs to be developed in tandem with their growing symbolic understanding. Within all the play structures, the causal significance (underlying purpose or intention) of the activity is described, to enable the teacher to focus explicitly (or implicitly) on the underlying patterns that explain the sequence of events in the play episode.

Intervention in play with children with autism

It is not the case that children with autism are deficient in their ability to play, simply because they appear to lack the drive to do so. Rather, they need to be *enabled* to play creatively and *motivated* to do so. The Options approach (Kaufman 1976, 1994) emphasises the 'three Es' to characterise playful relationships with children with autism: Energy, Enthusiasm and Excitement. Williams (1996), an adult with autism, advises this may be too confrontational, and advocates a more oblique, less invasive approach. Significantly, she suggests music, art and movement as particularly appropriate media for building interaction, as they offer flexibility in structure and degree of involvement required. Progress is therefore not just in the ability to play in more complex ways, but is seen in the social dimensions – small gains in concentration, involvement with others and greater confidence in acitivities (Clethero 2001, Purdie 1996, Peter 1996a).

The key to unlocking the latent play potential of children with autism is in interaction with sensitive adults. As Duffy (1998) says, 'our role is to:

- create conditions within which children are inspired to be creative and imaginative;
- develop children's creativity and imagination through our interactions with them' (p. 95).

Creating conditions for purposeful play

Before a child can share experiences and join in with the thoughts and feelings of other children, a wealth of meaningful personal experience is required, through which relationships are mediated and attitudes towards oneself and the social world are formed. The child must become an 'emotional shareholder' in the business of social interaction! It is possible to structure early learning experiences to allow children with autism at any stage of communication to develop social play and gain pleasure from the sharing of exciting play episodes.

Early caregiver–child interactions are characterized by a predictable structure based on mutually understood key moments, which the infant learns to anticipate and sequence, as in the peek-a-boo example in Chapter 1. It is through 'tweaking' these key moments – varying these early games – that the young child learns not only that new meanings can be shared and developed, but also that things can be different. It is the security and constraints of the structure, paradoxically, that enable new meaningful constructions to be made. Through structured play contexts where anticipated responses are varied, children with autism too may discover how representations can be manipulated.

Prevezer (2000) identifies the particular importance of certain preverbal conversation skills as providing foundations for the development of positive relationships with children with autism:

- *shared attention* – attending together to something else, making contact with one another;
- *turn-taking* – as in conversational 'give and take', timing utterances and movements to alternate with another person, regulated listening, watching, anticipating and using eye-contact;
- *imitation* – reinforcing (mirroring) a child's spontaneous reactions, as well as modelling appropriate play responses;
- *reciprocation* – both partners being able to lead and respond in a balanced 'dialogue'.

Initially, it may be that the attention of a child with autism can only be captured by fairly close imitation. However, as Prevezer (2000) points out, exact imitation of a child's sounds and actions can risk leading to a degree of undesirable rigidity; instead, she cites Stern (1985) in expanding on the notion of *affect attunement*. This entails the teacher capturing the essence of a child's movement, rhythm or sound in order to express a shared *feeling*, rather than pure imitation that only reflects superficial shared behaviour. 'Affect attunement' therefore, will involve the careful adjustment of an activity to take account of the preferences and sensibilities of the child.

It is crucial that play contexts are structured at an appropriate level, so that children learn to flex the mind and make creative choices and decisions within boundaries that feel secure. This may then underpin their confidence in coping with change and contribute to the generation of possibilities. Chapter 2 described the key conditions for facilitating purposeful play experiences in children with autism:

- structure;
- interests;
- affect.

Crucially, social experiences and language have to be made meaningful for children with autism, who are not driven by an active search for meaning. Interactive approaches will promote quality relationships and provide intrinsic motivation through play experiences in which the child can safely explore and experiment with possibilities within clearly defined boundaries, facilitated by the sensitive guidance of the teacher. Not only will this entail monitoring play possibilities within a *structure*, but also the child's interest levels in the activity, and whether these are waning. There needs to be a finely tuned balance between the child's actual and potential play ability within an activity, with sufficient challenge: if the level of incongruity of the activity with the child's competence (actual and/or latent) is too great – or too small – the child with autism may easily lose interest.

As indicated earlier, obsessive *interests* of children with autism in some circumstances can provide a powerful personal relevance, and be harnessed as a starting point to promote play, as a shared, meaningful focus. Children with autism will find it easier to relate to (and therefore be more motivated by) concrete, visible items, and will have to learn to understand symbols and representational forms – their actual capacity for more abstract thought can be deceptively lower than their other developmental abilities might suggest (Peeters 2000). Crozier (1997) highlights the importance of children understanding the point of an activity, as well as opportunities for the child to exercise creativity and make decisions. He also notes how novelty, surprise, incongruity, fantasy and humour can enhance motivation and the appeal of an activity. A proviso for children with autism, is that these are all carefully judged, in order not to challenge boundaries too quickly: timing the introduction of change or the unexpected should be sensitively paced.

Nevertheless, a further key element for play intervention with children with autism would seem to be a high level of *affective engagement*. Newson (2000) discusses use of humour to enable flexibility and social empathy in children with Asperger's syndrome. Similarly, Prevezer (2000) indicates how use of humour, suspense, excitement and emotional warmth are essential to play experiences with children with autism, but that levels of emotional arousal need to be carefully regulated. Interestingly, Lillard (1994) noted that when real or imaginary events trigger highly charged emotional reactions, there is a resultant positive impact on a child's ability to access this information and to distinguish between reality and pretence. Sherratt (1999) also instances how melodrama (for example, excitability, fun, shock, despair, mock horror) can be used effectively with children with autism to emphasise the significance of an imaginary experience, and that this appears to have a motivating influence as well as helping children's symbolic understanding. The teacher needs to maintain a sensitive balance between not overwhelming a child and, at the same time, investing an experience with sufficient personal relevance by giving it affective resonance (Sherratt 2001; Peter 1994).

Interacting in the play process

Left to their own devices, children with autism will often resist the new, preferring to stick with the known and the predictable – their rigidity of thought, and difficulty in seeing potential in a situation, can result in obsessive, limited and ritualistic play behaviour. It can be a delicate issue, balancing their need for security with the familiar (yet which may offer no further challenge), with new experiences that risk the child feeling insecure and vulnerable; indeed, panic behaviour may ensue, resulting in a repertoire of avoidance strategies. Sometimes play can be a frustrating experience! Indeed, this sense of unease and discomfort is similar to the state of 'cognitive disequilibrium' mooted by Piaget, as the child's previous interpretation of the world is challenged by the assimilation of new information, and the child endeavours to accommodate it into a new perspective.

The responsibility of the teacher is to provide a stimulus (direct experiences, objects, artefacts, materials, a selection of ideas), and to make children aware of creative possibilities and to support their response. Hutt (1979) observed two stages in children's play as they 'get to grips' with new equipment or skills, before being able to use them creatively: firstly a stage of *epistemic play* as the child investigates possibilities, and secondly a stage of *ludic play* as the child practises newfound possibilities. Duffy (1998) cites a useful four-stage model of the creative process proposed by Cecil *et al.* (1985), as a means to support children as they

	Play Process	Child	Teacher
Structured Context	**Curiosity**	What is it?	■ **Capturing interest and attention** ■ **Providing stimulus (play materials)**
	Exploration	What can it do?	■ **Encouraging and reinforcing initiative** ■ **Demonstrating and modelling other possibilities** ■ **Supporting imitation by the child**
	Consolidation	What can I do with this?	■ **Reminding (prompting recall) of the play experience** ■ **Sensitively supporting the child practising the play strategy** ■ **Reviewing the play experience with the child**
Free Play Context	**Creativity**	What else can I do with this?	■ **Providing play materials within a defined play space** ■ **Prompting recall of previous play experience** ■ **Discussing play intention** ■ **Being available to support as necessary – especially a new development & initiative** ■ **Evaluating the experience with the child**

Figure 3.1 Supporting the play process

endeavour to master an activity. This can offer a framework – an underpinning for planning – for developing play experiences with children with autism, that involve equipment, materials, ideas or a combination of some or all of these. Figure 3.1 builds on this model, to clarify the teacher's role in supporting the child at different stages of the play process.

Figure 3.1 also incorporates an additional useful model for supporting children with autism in both structured and free play contexts: the High/Scope plan–do–review principle (as advocated by proponents of the High/Scope Curriculum, founded by Weikart, then Director of Special Education in Michigan, USA, in 1961). This is based on the notion that a child will learn most effectively when experiences are provided that are in tune with his or her level of development, are initiated by the child and enable the child to reflect on his or her own interests (Mitchell 1994):

1. *Planning* – discussing and shaping a child's intention.
2. *Doing* – enabling a child to achieve an intention through sensitive support.
3. *Reviewing* – reflecting on the activity with the child with a view to next time.

Structured play experiences are important *not* just as an end in themselves, but also as preparation for genuinely creative, spontaneous activity. It is possible to conceive children's developing play as a spiral, where the teacher sensitively constructs a continuing alternating series of free-play and structured play opportunities. In this way, the child can re-visit a play experience, each time more informed and with a gradually developing (and strengthening) ability to engage purposefully (see Figure 3.2).

Spontaneous play is most likely to arise from recall of direct experiences and

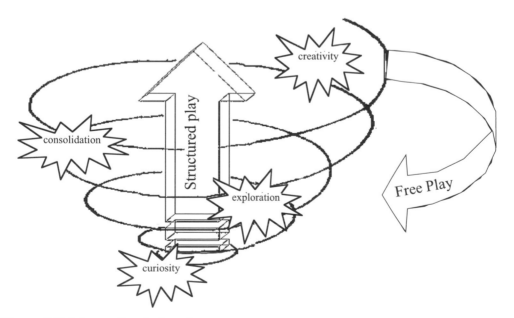

Figure 3.2 Intervention in the play process

previous play scenarios, rather than projecting into fantasy or an activity that has not been personally experienced. Children with autism, to greater or lesser degrees, will struggle to find an inner sense of resourcefulness or to make connections with a previous experience. This may need to be bridged through using visual cues – objects, photographs, pictures, video. In order to engage in purposeful, spontaneous play, children with autism may also need to be supported in recalling their emotional engagement with a previous play experience. This is due to their particular difficulty with personal autobiographical memory – a limited awareness of themselves caught up in an experience, and consequently a more restricted developing sense of 'self' (Jordan and Powell 1995).

Children with autism should be encouraged to plunder! They need to take what they know as a basis for their pretence, and then invent some more (DfES 2001a); for example:

- retelling a familiar story;
- changing a known story;
- mixing ingredients from different stories;
- retelling anecdotes.

The teacher will need to be sensitive not to over-cue, as this may result in the child with autism overriding the development, and reverting instead to the narrative as known (as Daniel did in Chapter 2, when presented with a familiar trigger for a play sequence). Introducing a more flexible attitude to narrative will have to be carefully paced, through sensitive use of a few elements (objects, props) of a familiar play sequence that can be used in a more pivotal way. The child will also need to be explicitly talked through the experience, perhaps plotting out an alternative play sequence using a storyboard approach (refer to the example of Daniel in Chapter 2). The teacher may need to support the child in developing the play episode by demonstrating (and sensitively prompting) possible ways to develop the emerging story and a basic narrative structure; for example:

- deciding on the characters, opening setting and activity;
- developing what is happening (something occurs – change of scene? introduction of a new character or event?);
- introducing tension – a problem or dilemma (for example, finding something hidden, making a discovery, a surprise, a difficulty, a shortage, etc.);
- finding a resolution to a tricky situation.

Playing spontaneously

As indicated in Chapter 2, in purposeful, spontaneous pretend play, the child brings together affective and cognitive recognition of play possibilities within the constraints of the particular context. This triggers a self-generated desire in the child to pursue and continue the activity, and will facilitate meaningful engagement and quality play. Engagement in pretend play helps strengthen connections in the brain, and oils manipulation of linguistic and social concepts: the free-flow mental processes and release for neurotransmitters allow the child to wallow in ideas, and to develop a fluency and fluidity of thought. However, this will be dependent on certain conditions, such as:

- a reason to generate a novel idea – the activity has to be inherently appealing to the particular child;
- a wealth of first-hand experience – the child will need a fund of ideas based on direct participation in a range of life situations;
- a fluency in modifying representations – the more the child plays, the more the mind will increase its flexibility and generate new possibilities from an informed awareness of a range of options;
- often having someone to be spontaneous with – this needs to be the right person, at first usually an adult or older, more experienced child, who is able to attune to the child;
- the process being pleasurable – it needs to be fun and humorous.

Humour is a characteristic of play from the earliest stages of development – for example, even a baby may engage in 'concrete modifications' by picking up a cup and putting it in his or her dinner, looking at the caregiver for a reaction! This breaks away from the normal narrative 'cups are for drinking'. In doing this, a 'humorous' and spontaneous modification has been made, in which the child creates a new narrative – 'cups are for putting in dinner'. In so doing, the child demonstrates the ability to hold two representations in mind at the same time, one of reality and the other of the imagination. The child shows not only a functional understanding of cups, but also a symbolic recognition of what cups can be made into. This is a similar process to that seen in early symbolic play; also the way a child combines words into novel constructions in early speech.

Structured play involves the scaffolding of both social and physical constructions; it is useful to be able to separate these components in relation to children with autism. Whatever the child's level of language, the teacher will need to make a judgement regarding the level of *social demand* to the play activity: whether the child with autism can accept (and therefore benefit from) a high social structure or a low social structure. Activities that use a high social structure include: modelled play, 'snakes and ladders', lotto, musical chairs, cat-and-mouse chase, or throwing and catching a ball. Activities that use a low social structure include: home corner play, toy cars and garage, adventure playgrounds, pen and paper, dough, clay, rough-and-tumble play or construction sets (for example, Lego or Mobilo). The social structure refers to the demands and challenges made by the presence or involvement of other people in an activity, not to the organisation and sequencing of the physical objects and materials.

Some children are highly intolerant of either high or low forms of social structuring. Children who prefer to work to 'their own agenda' may need an approach that uses low social structure. Other children may not play at all unless the teacher uses a high social structure and has an expectation that the children will participate. In normally developing children, activities that use a low social structure are more likely to promote spontaneity in their play. For children with autism, this assumption cannot be made, and a careful balance must be found. Where the teacher is unsure of the best social structure to use, it is often better to start with high structure, then repeat the activity with a lower social structure. The best approach is to remain flexible, as the level of social structure required may vary from one play opportunity to another, depending on the child's mood and the preceding events of the day.

As the child's language develops, so does the sophistication of the child's play potential, with implications for the *physical structuring* of an activity. A child at a preverbal stage of development will be able to engage in exploratory play with objects. It follows that once the child is mentally able to ascribe a label to an object ('cup') and refer to it when not there ('ball' to mean 'I want my ball – where is it?'), a basic capacity for representational thought and symbolisation will be evident. A child who is able to connect two or three meaningful words in an utterance ('cup – table' for 'put the cup on the table') will be capable of sustaining a brief play sequence. As simple utterances develop into more complex ones, so the child may be able to sustain a longer episode of pretend play.

The following stages of play development may be identified (see Figure 3.6, page 53):

- *Sensori-motor* – exploration of the different properties of the world by acting on it, possibly through touching, mouthing, biting, smelling, tasting, hitting, kicking, running, crawling, jumping.
- *Relational* – exploration of the relationship between properties of selected objects; for example, by inserting, building, grouping or associating them in different ways.
- *Functional* – gaining pleasure from using objects as they are supposed to be used; for example, making a toy dog bark, or pretending to drink from a cup.
- *Symbolic* – gaining pleasure from using objects within a simple sequence and in a way that stands for something else; for example, pretending a cup contains a very hot drink, making a cardboard box into a pretend camera or imagining that there is a crocodile in the bath.
- *Sociodramatic* – consciously acting out social interactions, usually involving two or more people in a sequence of actions that form a simple story based on

everyday occurrences; for example, pretending to cook a meal for a visitor.

- *Themed fantasy* – highly imaginative and creative pretence within a dynamic narrative. Typically, children's play is both interactive and spontaneous.

In sociodramatic play, children deliberate and work out what to do 'as if' they were particular people. In themed fantasy (spontaneous imaginary play), they move from that position, to a state of thinking 'as if' they are those people (Kitson 1994). While the child is aware that it is make-believe, nevertheless the feelings experienced are real. Sensitive adult intervention can extend and enhance the children's pretence while still ensuring their 'ownership' of the experience: the teacher can facilitate the development of their play, and make learning potential within the experience more precise. By working alongside the children on the inside of the developing narrative, the teacher is able to stimulate, motivate and facilitate the play. In this way, the children are supported in working at a deeper level than they would otherwise achieve in free-play contexts, and are enabled through the structured play situation to engage in play behaviour at a level beyond their cognitive norm (Vygotsky 1978; Kitson 1994).

Teaching children with autism to play

The following points are particularly important in teaching children with autism to develop their ability to play:

- *Children with autism are more likely to develop their play within a narrative structure. This may be provided externally (for example, modelling a traditional fairy story), constructed internally (for example, based on a favourite video) or generated internally (for example, 'I am a wizard, I can do magic').*
- *Play should be meaningful for the child. The child must align his or her thoughts, feelings and perceptions about an event or object in the play. This attitude towards play can be brought about by engaging the children within shared affective experiences or by productively involving their area or object of interest within the play.*
- *Teachers should lead the child's development of play from the restricted to the spontaneous, from the asocial to the socially interactive and from sensori-motor to sociodramatic and themed fantasy play.*
- *Children with autism need to be assessed using free-play observation* and *a structured assessment in order to make realistic judgements about their abilities in play.*

In order to gauge an appropriate level of challenge, the teacher needs a clear idea of the usual play behaviour of the child with autism (as in a free-play context) and his or her potential capability within a structured play opportunity. It is important, therefore, that this disparity is accurately assessed, in order for the teacher to construct a way forward through appropriate play contexts.

Assessing play of children with autism

The play of children with autism is often considered problematic to assess accurately because the level of their unprompted play is frequently much lower than their other abilities, including language. As there is a close association between play and verbal comprehension, an assessment that shows no spontaneous play in a verbal child can cause some confusion. Similarly, the lack of spontaneity and creativity that children with autism often show in their play often results in no play during the course of an observation, and adds to the difficulty.

However, it is clear that in a very structured setting, children with autism are able to demonstrate play behaviours at a much higher level than when they play freely. This is an important point in teaching pretend play to children with autism. Children with autism are impaired in their ability to construct novel acts of play and construct a narrative that sequences these coherently in an unstructured setting. An accurate assessment of the child's ability to symbolise in a structured setting enables the teacher to scaffold a narrative sequence that can free the child to use his or her underlying abilities. It is critically important for those teaching children with autistic spectrum disorders to recognise which play stage they are *able* to use in a supportive environment, as this represents their latent potential.

Watching children in a free-play setting, the observer may not see any real difference in the quality of their play. In a supportive, structured setting, the child may be capable of significantly higher play levels – it is this information that teachers need to know. In a group of children, it is necessary for teachers to appreciate that while all the children may seem to be playing at a sensori-motor stage, some may have the potential to play at relational, functional or symbolic levels.

It is also possible to make judgements about the *affective engagement* of children with autism that are useful in planning future play opportunities. Children with autism can sometimes show unusual reactions to a stimulus. For example, instead of showing pleasure and joining in with other children singing 'Happy birthday to you' at a party, some may show a negative reaction and become distressed. Positive and negative levels of affective engagement are listed below. It is crucial that teachers are aware of and sensitive to possible affective triggers and tolerances for each individual child within a teaching group.

Levels of positive affective engagement:

- observes others engaged in play;
- is attracted by the emotional responses of others;
- shares affective moments with others;
- unintentionally creates affective moments within a play narrative;

- deliberately creates affective moments within a play narrative in order to share meaning with others.

Levels of negative affective engagement:

- tolerates unobtrusive affective responses of others;
- becomes agitated by affective responses of others but continues to observe;
- demonstrates a different affective response to that of the others; for example, laughs when another child cries;
- shows a pronounced idiosyncratic affective response compared to that of the others; for example, runs away holding ears or becomes aggressive;
- memory of a previous experience prevents the child from participating.

The following assessments provide valuable information for different purposes.

Assessment schedules

Two standardised assessment schedules for play are generally available, and can be used to ascertain a developmental age level for children's play. Both are straightforward and easy to use, and complement one another:

- The Symbolic Play Test (Lowe and Costello 1989) is particularly useful for assessing children who are beginning to develop *functional play*. This test uses representational objects such as a toy bed, pillow, chair and doll to assess spontaneous nonverbal play activities in a structured situation.
- The Test of Pretend Play (Lewis and Boucher 1998) offers a sound analytic framework for assessing those children capable of *symbolic play*. It is designed to assess this verbally or nonverbally in structured or unstructured contexts, using a range of largely non-representational objects. These include a blue cloth square, a box and some cotton wool. The test is in four sections, and assesses the child's ability to play symbolically: firstly with everyday objects, secondly with a representational toy and non-representational objects, thirdly with a representational toy alone, and finally by pretending to be something, do something or have something that is not really there.

Observation schedules

A straightforward questionnaire to assist in observations of children with autism at play is provided by Beyer and Gammeltoft (2000). This gives a useful list of questions to assist the teacher towards *understanding the child with autism in play*.

Pertinent questions are asked about:

- the child's use of materials, social behaviour and play stage during free play;

- the social involvement between teacher and child in imitation, turn-taking and tickle games;
- the child's play with dolls, including recognition of the need for structured questions to contrast with a free-play observation.

A much fuller observation profile is provided by Cumine *et al.* (2000). This asks a series of important questions that would result in an informative and autism-relevant summary of the child's *social and play skills*. It looks in some depth at interactions in play, functional, symbolic, fantasy and social play. It also provides a list of questions that specifically look at play and flexibility when the child is outdoors, in the home corner or playing with sand/water or toy cars and trains. These form a rich addition to the child's observation profile. The profile asks for information on:

- *social interaction* – including spontaneous use of gaze, spontaneous maintenance of proximity, imitation, turn-taking, initiating, emotional expression and understanding and development of self;
- *communication* – understanding of simple verbal and non-verbal approaches, strategies for meeting needs, engagement in social interaction and joint attention strategies;
- *play and imagination* – manipulative, organisational, constructional, and cause and effect play.

Assessing play capability

The following short schedule provides questions that attempt to identify better the child's *capabilities* to play (see Figure 3.3). It does this by comparing free-play and structured play observations of the child's play behaviour (see Figures 3.4 and 3.5). The information resulting from these feeds directly into planning for structured teaching and should be used with the 'play structures for children with autism' in Appendix A. These provide suggested frameworks for teaching play at different stages of development with children who have autism. It is intended that this assessment should complement the tests and observation schedules described above.

Play structures

Although many children with autism make very slow progress in their development through the play stages, it is possible to increase this rate of development rapidly by using appropriate teaching structures. These play structures attempt to guide the child into developing and using his or her play potential. They are not intended to train children to perform behavioural routines. Instead, they aim to provide a

Assessment Schedule for Play Capability
1 The child is given a plastic bucket, a car, a small doll and some boxes. The teacher watches the child in a free-play situation for five minutes or until an observation is made and notes this.
2 The teacher identifies the highest play stage behaviour that the child used. Which example was the nearest to the child's highest level behaviour: sensori-motor, relational, functional, symbolic, sociodramatic or themed fantasy play?
3 The teacher then begins the Structured Play Assessment for the highest play stage identified in the Free-Play Observation. The prompts given in the structured play situation are aimed at a higher level than the child demonstrated in the free-play context.
4 The teacher notes the result of this intervention and interprets the outcomes in terms of higher levels of play.
5 The highest level of play is identified as a starting point for planning structured, teacher-led contexts for developing the child's play. The teacher identifies suggested play structures (Appendix A) suitable for children able to play at that level.
6 If the child demonstrates only sensori-motor play in the Structured Play Assessment, he or she should be offered play structures at 'level 1: extension'. Other children should be offered play structures at levels suggested in the 'implications' section of the assessment.

Figure 3.3 Assessment schedule for play capability

Free-Play Observation	
Sensori-Motor	The child takes the objects to his or her mouth, throws them across the room or spins car wheels. Play focuses on the sensory qualities of the materials.
Implication	Use the sensori-motor play structured play assessment.
Relational	The child builds a tower or fills the bucket with boxes and toys or organises the materials in some way.
Implication	Use the relational play structured play assessment.
Functional	The child takes the toy car and runs it along the floor or removes doll's clothing.
Implication	Use the functional play structured play assessment.
Symbolic	The child takes the car and a small box and creates a car crash or puts a box in the bucket and says, 'boat' or puts the doll in the bucket and washes the doll's face as if in the bath.
Implication	Use the symbolic play structured play assessment.

Figure 3.4 Free-play observation

Structured Play Assessment	
Sensori-Motor	The teacher hides the doll under the bucket and then lifts it saying 'Boo'. The teacher fills the bucket and shakes it to make it rattle.
Example & comment	*The child may show increased interest in the materials in this structured setting. The child may attempt to imitate the teacher's behaviour or impose some structure on the materials.*
Implication	Plan play structures suitable for relational play.
Relational	The teacher takes the doll and makes it climb up a mountain of the bucket and boxes or the doll sits on the car and makes 'brum-brum' noises.
Example & comment	*The child used actions with the car or doll that were <u>appropriate</u>. The child used the car to drive around the edge of the table.*
Implication	Plan play structures suitable for functional play.
Functional	The teacher says 'car in garage' or 'doll in house'.
Example & comment	*The child put the car or the doll in a box and may understand the use of symbols in structured play. The child put the doll in a box and said 'sleep' and may be capable of <u>symbolic play</u> in a structured setting.*
Implication	Plan play structures suitable for early symbolic play.
Symbolic	The teacher says, 'What else can you do with this car/doll?'
Example & comment	*The child was able to create a different and <u>novel</u> symbolic act as a result of the question, which could be <u>spontaneous</u> and imaginative.*
Implication	Plan play structures suitable for sociodramatic or themed fantasy play (see interactive and spontaneous play structures).

Figure 3.5 Structured play assessment

'scaffold' to allow children with autism to use their symbolic capability in a meaningful way. Within each stage of development, some of these sample play structures may be appropriate for children who are capable of spontaneous pretend play, but still have difficulties in flexible and coherent thinking. Appendix A contains a number of suggested play structures that can be used to develop play.

It is possible to think of learning to play in terms of a progression from narrow or repetitive play to spontaneous, imaginative play. In Figure 3.6, possible play structures are shown as circles along a continuum for progression. These play structures may be used to allow the child's own play to emerge. At the earliest point on this progression, children are often engaged in highly repetitive play that has been copied or is insular and idiosyncratic. At this point in their development, children often require a high level of structure if they are to extend their play. As children progress, over time, the structure may become less overt, and play options broadened.

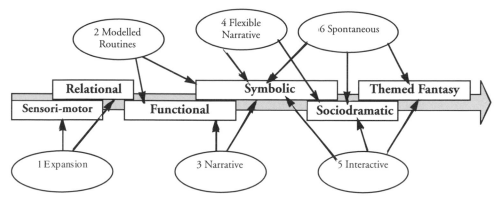

Figure 3.6 Progression in play

1. *Expansion* – attempts to extend the child's play by working on his or her interests in a sensitive manner; the teacher offers additional opportunities in line with the child's interests to extend thinking.
2. *Modelled routines* – development of short routines with materials that may involve two or three different actions.
3. *Narrative* – play routines are embedded within a familiar narrative form.
4. *Flexible narrative* – the narrative framework is more open and opportunities for variation are encouraged.
5. *Interactive* – the narrative is developed through the interactions of two or more players.
6. *Spontaneous* – the child works within a narrative and responds with increasing flexibility, imagination and spontaneity, leading towards sociodramatic and themed fantasy play.

In the following examples, play structures 1–6 are described by relating the goals of increasing expansion, flexibility, narrative, imagination and spontaneity to the play of individual children. Although some of these structures are used with individuals and others with groups of children, they are described in terms of one particular child with autism.

Play Structure 1: Expansion

In the first play structure, the intention is to expand the child's own interests in materials or social relationships. Paradoxically, joining the child in a preferred routine can be a useful starting point for expanding possibilities – building a point of contact in something that has emotional significance to the child. Children with autism at this level tend to play repetitively, repeating sequences or using very limited expressions of play; for example, they may line up objects, spin wheels or reconstruct jigsaws. Even children who are capable of play at higher levels will often spend long periods of time in repetitive play.

These are useful play structures to use with children with autism who are operating at *sensori-motor* and *relational* play stages. It may also be used with children at higher stages who would benefit from developing a less restrictive focus. They may gain from revisiting and consolidating their understanding that they may generate play-like routines as a focus for joint attention and the development of a shared meaning with another person.

Andrew liked to complete formboards in which he would insert shaped wooden pieces into a board. He liked posting boxes and simple jigsaws. Andrew liked cars and aeroplanes and particularly enjoyed playing with trains. He would concentrate for long periods of time on moving a train along the track while his head lay close to the railway line. Much of Andrew's interest in the toys was at a sensory or emergent relational level. He performed very similar actions with the toys each time he was given them.

The play structure used with Andrew tried to develop his understanding of the relational aspects of his play and led towards opportunities to take this into early functional play. As Andrew was unhappy if anyone interfered with his train track before or after he built it, the teacher built a separate train track next to him on the floor. Andrew was allowed to join with the teacher's track and play with the new train engines, but did not take any of these materials back with him. As Andrew became used to working with the superior materials that the teacher used, the teacher was able to introduce variations to the shape, size and construction of the track layout. After several weeks of changing the layout, the teacher was able to introduce other features into the layout (a bridge, lights, a railway station and locating a farm set next to the track). Andrew became less interested in his original train set and started to share the building with the teacher.

Through this process, Andrew was able to extend his play and started to share aspects of this with the teacher. He had reduced his intolerance of change and had started to recognise some value in the opportunities that the new train track afforded.

Play Structure 2: Modelled routines

In this second play structure, children may extend their understanding of the world and the way we relate to it by developing simple routines. This structure uses modelled or imitated teaching techniques to develop the child's play, with the teacher explicitly showing the child how to perform a particular action. The teacher should also demonstrate some expressions of pleasure in his or her own play. This structure may be useful with children capable of *relational play*, and lead them towards more *functional* and *early symbolic play*.

Ellie showed little interest in using toys or watching the play of other children. She was reasonably interested in the toys in the role-play area, although this was usually a fleeting moment of inspection rather than using them to play. She would not show spontaneous play, although on occasions she would find a doll and a spoon and commence feeding, giving the doll a few mouthfuls of pretend food. Ellie was able to perform pretend actions or make a teddy bear perform them if somebody asked her. When an adult asked her to make 'teddy sleep', she would manipulate teddy's arms to make a pillow and lay him down. Ellie was able to perform some well-established routines and incorporate these into a few symbolic acts, although most of her play was at an early functional level.

A play structure for Ellie was used that built on her relational and functional use of items in play situations, by teaching her additional routines and flexibility in using these. Ellie was shown how to use a number of household toys from the role-play area. She was shown how to use the iron and how to fold clothes. Later she was shown how to wash the dishes with pretend water, give dolly a bath and how to put on dolly's clothes.

Ellie's play developed in its range of different routines, although remained unspontaneous and largely unsymbolic. However, after a year's structured play intervention, she did develop some flexibility in using the same materials in slightly different ways; for example, she was able to dress dolly in different clothes and she was able to feed her using different crockery and utensils.

Play Structure 3: Narrative

This play structure encourages children to fit together the play acts into short sequences or scripts. These are tied into a simple narrative form during the process of play or may be used to act out an established story. Many children with autism prefer the second form of narrative: stories, movies and particularly videos may be very useful narrative frameworks, and provide the stimulus for this type of structure. This structure is designed for children capable of simple *functional* and *emergent symbolic* play.

Ross was a lively child, bursting with energy and intensely involved in his own interests, which often appeared obsessive. Ross did have some language, although much of this had little communicative power: he tended to relate phrases and sentences that probably came from music, rhymes, television or video. His speech was often not directed toward anyone else and appeared to be a commentary on his thoughts or actions. In the free-play observation Ross had not used the objects to play and squashed the box instead. In the structured play schedule, Ross crashed the car into the bucket until the bucket fell off the table. He was assessed as using simple functional play.

The play structure attempted to develop sequences of pretend play actions within a familiar narrative. This also provided a foundation for communication as speech acts and actions are used in similar ways to represent the thought sequences within a shared narrative. Ross had been to see the film 'Tarzan' at the cinema and had greatly enjoyed it. The teacher found a leafy branch and tied it to the table so that it overhung the tabletop. Pieces of string were fastened to the branches so they hung down like vines. Ross was given a male doll figure and invited to play Tarzan. Ross became annoyed by the arrangement and pulled the 'tree' to pieces, throwing twigs and leaves to every part of the room.

Two days later, Ross had found some cotton thread and was sticking lengths of it to the underside of a shelf. He became annoyed once more because he was unable to tie the thread to the doll's wrists. Later in the week he re-used a piece of sticky tape to attach a shoelace to the doll hand and had jammed the other end between two tables. He was now happily prodding the doll and watching him swing like a pendulum between the tables. One month later, Ross was observed playing with a box full of cuddly toys including the male doll, all of which had been amply sticky-taped to a broom handle. Ross then raised the broom, before letting it crash to the floor.

Ross was starting to develop his own play. It is probable that he had been using aspects of play prior to this, but that this was undisclosed and uncommunicated. His play was at a functional level, and he showed a perseverance to play but required the correct setting and structures to enable this. Although Ross was only beginning to sequence actions, there was coherence to his play and the beginnings of a simple narrative. He also showed the possibility of early symbolic play.

Play Structure 4: Flexible narrative

This play structure uses objects (representational or non-representational) or verbal prompts to promote a more *flexible approach to play* in a developing narrative. It is designed to modify established narratives or to develop an original narrative through variations on the expected, using those props or prompts at the appropriate moment. This play structure is most suitable for children who can employ some functional or symbolic play.

Sophie was a quiet and relatively passive child, who liked reading, although it was difficult to assess her understanding of the text. Sophie could understand simple and straightforward requests, and had been assessed as having an understanding of spoken language at approximately three years. Although she did not play spontaneously she was able to take part in acting out simple storybook characters. In the free-play observation Sophie had not used the objects to play and simply sat and looked at them. In the structured play observation, Sophie started on the relational assessment point and then went onto the functional assessment question. She copied the modelled routine of the doll walking up the mountain of boxes. When asked if she could put the doll in her house, Sophie placed the doll inside a box and put the bucket on top of the box. She was assessed as being suitable for using symbolic play structures.

The play structure for Sophie used her ability to understand language by involving her in the story of the 'Three Billy Goats Gruff'. In this Sophie was asked to be a goat and walk across the bridge when it was her turn (a piece of blue cloth was used as a prop for the river and a mask was used to indicate her role as a goat and provide some extra motivation). The teacher acted as narrator and endeavoured to describe the behaviour of the children in terms of the storyline. The teacher then explained that the storyline would change: this time, the goats would cross the bridge and the troll would chase them rather than block their way. On a future occasion, the troll asked for a penny each time the goats crossed. Finally the goats went across the bridge and took a picnic to share with the troll.

Several weeks later, instead of starting from a familiar narrative, the teacher explained that a new story would be used. A rocket was made from some upturned tables and space helmets from thin card. The props that had been brought into the play guided each new step in this adventure to the moon. Sophie was able to adapt her behaviour in line with the other children in this group: she could brace herself on take-off, float airily on the space-walk and swim through the ocean upon splashdown.

In this double example, Sophie had been able to accommodate changes to the narrative as the play proceeded. She was not distressed by this, but engaged with it in a flexible way. The prompts were provided by objects introduced into the play, the actions of several other children and prompts given by the narrator.

Play Structure 5: Interactive

This is a dynamic play structure that builds on the previous levels, and uses *interactive* prompts to increase flexibility in the child's play. This flexibility originates in the play of another person, who may be a child or adult with whom the child with autism will actively engage in the play. This structure is most effective with children who can use functional play competently and have at least the beginnings of symbolic play.

William was often in trouble with other children because he would touch and prod and occasionally nip them under the table. He recognised how to tease the other children and was entertained by their responses. William used a variety of mannerisms when he became agitated or excited; these included flapping his hands, slapping his face and stamping his left foot on the floor. William was passionately interested in a restricted and very idiosyncratic range of objects. However this interest was not totally obsessive, and he did develop these interests if he was given the opportunities. William was interested in kitchen furniture and particularly refrigerators. In the free-play assessment, William was thought to have used some functional play when he moved the car across the tabletop. Unfortunately he became so engrossed in the fact that he could not open the car doors, that he did not demonstrate very much play. In the structured assessment, William was able to use a symbolic representation in putting the car in bed with the doll and saying 'the car is sleeping'.

In this play structure, William was teamed with an older boy, Joe, who also had autism. Joe really liked washing machines: he loved the way they rotated and the sounds they made when they were starting or stopping. William and Joe were given a room equipped with cardboard boxes of different sizes and a variety of junk materials. Playing independently at first, William and Joe explored the boxes. Joe had inserted a plastic jar into a box; he pushed some strips of cloth into the jar and turned it round as if it were a washing machine. On hearing Joe's excitement, William looked at the washing machine and attempted to remove the strips of cloth. Joe was outraged and pushed William away. William came back with more strips of cloth and said 'washing machine, put clothes in the washing machine'. Joe allowed this and William pushed the material into the jar. Encouraged by his success, William continued to fill the washing machine until it was full and Joe continued to turn the jar round. Having won over Joe's confidence, William started to insert some plastic tubing and paper drinking straws into the cardboard box. Some of these lined the box and some poked out of the back. Several minutes later, William had converted the washing machine into a refrigerator. William removed selected strips of cloth and handed some of these to Joe. Some he put to his mouth, saying 'mmm . . . sausage, lettuce, mmm . . . chocolate'. Joe seemed a little perplexed by this change but reluctantly went along with it.

In this play structure, William had started to interact with Joe because William wanted the washing machine. William was able to use a symbolic representation of clothing and later converted this into food. The play in this instance had been enhanced by grouping the two boys together.

Play Structure 6: Spontaneous

In this final play structure, teaching attempts to promote the use of *spontaneous*, internally generated play in the child with autism. This requires the child to go beyond thinking of another routine, to follow or respond to a prompt or object. It requires the child to create a symbolic act that they have not used or imitated previously. The child may respond to a particular feature of an object or be stimulated to think in a particular way by someone else's comment. The result of this must be the production of an act of pretence that is novel to that particular child, and should reflect the child's intent to pretend (even if he or she is not aware of this).

Jamie was always very uncomfortable with changes in his daily life. He insisted on sitting in the same chair and coming to school by the same taxi route. Although his speech was clear, he barely spoke unless it was to shout at the other children. Jamie's understanding of spoken language was difficult to assess but was between 2 and 2.5 years. Jamie had excellent fine motor control and sometimes liked to balance objects. Earlier in the year, Jamie had stood 50 pencils on their flat ends to create a fence around a toy castle. This re-created a picture that he had seen in a history book. In the free-play observation Jamie had looked in the boxes but did not engage in play activities. In the structured assessment, he had cooperated with the teacher's requests at a functional play level but did not use any novel play constructions.

The chosen play structure for Jamie required the teaching staff to respond quickly and dynamically. Jamie had watched a video about a huge iron giant who was quite frightening at first and was sad at the end of the film. Jamie was highly animated during the film and had sometimes jumped up and down in his chair shouting at the images.

The following day Jamie started to construct something using several pencils and some sticky-tape that he had acquired from other children around the table. The teacher facilitated this by putting some extra pencils on the table along with a small box of found sources. After a few minutes it became clear that Jamie was constructing a man and that he was prodding it with a dead battery. Jamie lifted the man's head and made a creaking sound as he lowered it back to the ground; he repeated this several times before leaving the table. He then ran to the door and rattled the handle vigorously. Although Jamie was unable to explain his behaviour, the teacher opened the door and followed him to an adjoining room where art materials were stored. Jamie found a box immediately and emptied its contents. When he returned to his table, Jamie put the man into the box and sealed the lid. He carried the box to the coats and bags corner where he made a pile of coats on the floor. Taking great care, Jamie parted the coats and lowered the box into the hole that he had made. He covered over the box with coats and jumped to his feet, trembling with excitement. Crouching over the pile of coats he reached inside and opened the box lid. Taking the man into his hands he lifted him into the air before bounding across the room in renewed excitement.

It is unclear exactly what narrative Jamie was using in this episode. It seemed probable that it related to the previous day's video and his experience and interest in the Church and burials. However in discussing Jamie's play with his parents, it was clear that he had used this narrative before, although they were intrigued by the increasing complexity of his play. Jamie had almost certainly used several novel symbolic transformations in this play that were not directly imitated and in all probability were spontaneous.

Organisation of the play space

Although it is possible to set up a play situation in almost any environment, play can be enhanced by organising the play space to better suit the needs of children with autism. A good play space needs to recognise some of the problems that can adversely influence the quality of play. It should also consider features of the play space that can enhance the opportunities for developing play. In organising the play space teachers should consider the following points.

- There is a need for clarity of purpose: reduce objects from reach or view that are known to be a distraction or features that would produce irritation. This should allow the children to focus on the main points of the play.

- Sometimes allow children with autism to take their own favourite toys into the play space; these may act as triggers for the generation of meaningful play.
- Provide an appropriate amount of freedom in the organisation of furniture: provide clear guidance about the parameters of the play space, without restricting the opportunities for play.
- Have a range of props necessary for the play structure near to hand. These may be stored out of sight so that the teacher can use them to reinforce the narrative. Alternatively, the props can also be arranged within the children's reach so that they can be used as they wish.
- Keep a box of bits and pieces – miscellaneous items – close to hand. These should include found sources that do not readily suggest a particular play representation; for example, cardboard boxes, tubes, lengths of string, a ball of plasticine, and pieces of cloth in a range of sizes, colours, shapes and textures. These can be used in many varied ways and may afford greater opportunities for symbolic play.
- Provide opportunities for other children to watch the play episodes and invite them to join in the play using the same materials.
- Use photography and video to feed back some of the salient features emerging from the play episode. This can be used to focus the child's attention on the underlying causal patterns that draw together the otherwise disconnected sequence of actions.
- Using play with children with autism can introduce an element of unpredictability into the children's behaviour. It is sometimes useful to have available additional sensitive adult help. Teaching play is something that needs resourcing well, and should not be considered an activity that occupies children when they are not really working.
- The level of social intrusion needs to be judged by the teacher. Sitting children too near together or putting them in a position where they are unwillingly involved in a play episode should be avoided.

The following chapter shows how play may be extended through taking it into drama. This enables the teacher to provide structures and techniques that allow the children to examine their actions and those of others in terms of a shared or joint understanding of narrative. In this way, drama-in-education is of particular value to children with autism. The combination of the dynamic fluidity developed in play and the analytical framework of drama can help them to build powerful thinking processes that otherwise would not emerge.

CHAPTER 4

Taking Play into Drama

This chapter aims to extend the play continuum identified previously, through exploration of how play may be harnessed as a vehicle for deeper social learning and understanding. Taking make-believe play at its core, this chapter explores how drama may become a learning medium for children with autism. In this way, play behaviour demonstrated by children with autism is then a means to an end, not just an end in itself. The chapter presents an inclusive approach to using drama-in-education that is compatible with mainstream philosophy, and is appropriate for beginners in drama at all levels of ability, whatever their play starting point.

As with the framework developed earlier, here an order of teaching is presented that progressively challenges the level of spontaneous responses of the children, through use of drama structures that gradually widen the boundaries within which creative decisions may be made. In play-drama intervention, it is intended that the structured frameworks offered for both play and drama should be used in parallel: there is clear overlap (and distinct compatibility) with the kinds of activities suggested, but the teaching agenda is somewhat different.

Approaching drama

So what is the difference between make-believe play and drama? And does this mean that children who may not yet be demonstrating symbolic understanding through their observed play behaviours (whether in free-play or structured play situations as described earlier) cannot 'do drama'? Why bother with children who may seem to be on a 'hiding to nothing' when it comes to drama? What is the point of drama in education anyway, especially in relation to children with autism?

Essentially, drama at all levels of sophistication seeks to explore aspects of human experience – why people think and behave as they do – whether in the nursery classroom, on stage at the National Theatre or in a TV soap opera. Any drama (literally!) can put 'under the spotlight' and amplify moments when characters are on their mettle, often faced with some issue or dilemma to resolve; it is these moments that spur on the narrative. Drama enables us to focus on an analogous life-situation, in order to expose mechanisms by which decisions are arrived at, and subject to scrutiny the consequences of those actions, thoughts and behaviour. In educational contexts, this may offer learning opportunities for children to reflect explicitly on the viability of outcomes in the drama, and implications for similar situations in the real world. Drama then, is really about personal, social and emotional development as revealed through the narrative form. This is its learning potential for all children, but with a special poignancy in the case of those with autism, who are particularly challenged in this area.

Classroom drama operates at many levels: there is no getting away from it being a complex and challenging way of teaching. Teachers of drama at all levels across the educational spectrum are always worried to a greater or lesser degree about loss of physical control of the children and/or loss of control over ideas. The quality of learning in drama is crucially dependent on the opportunities presented by the teacher – an awesome responsibility! The problem for the teacher is that there will always be a part of the lesson that is unplanned (and therefore unpredictable), because drama at all levels depends on negotiated learning. Nevertheless, from the point of view of both the children and staff it can be a highly rewarding and *integrating* way of teaching and learning that builds naturally upon children's play instincts, and to which they bring their knowledge, skills and understanding of their world. The argument being proposed throughout this book is that children with autism may have latent ability to play, yet require structured intervention to develop their awareness of their play potential and the opportunities this may afford. Similarly, the approach to drama can be 'learning how to do it while doing it', rather than waiting for some magic point at which a child with autism otherwise may be deemed 'ready for drama'.

So how does it work? At the heart of the drama process lies make-believe play, which the teacher looks to challenge, by putting on the brakes, effectively to 'suspend the plot', in order to confront and focus participants with the implications of their actions and suggestions. The teacher looks to create a potential area of learning – provide a 'focusing lens' (Neelands 1984) – through the use of tension and a range of drama conventions, which give shape and structure to the developing drama experience. The unfolding drama is thus really on two levels: the 'play for the pupils' and the 'play for the teacher' (Gilham 1974), with the teacher seeking to set up situations – significant moments – for the participants to reflect on their behaviour in the safety of the make-believe. They are thus also empowered to take responsibility for their own learning, with a shift in the conventional teacher–pupil relationship. Taylor (1986) likens the drama process to the idea of creating Frankenstein's monster, involving a phase where the participants are consciously involved in creating a thing, which then becomes in some sense independent from them, and exerts forces that confront and challenge them!

Imagine the following scenario in a mainstream playground: children are engrossed in their own make-believe loosely based on the TV animation of 'The Flintstones'. 'Look out!' cries one child 'There's a dinosaur coming! Quick everyone, into the helicopter!' Without a problem, their unfolding story moves on seamlessly, with a 'quick-fix' solution thanks to modern technology, and without any second thought to possible hitches.

In the classroom situation however, the drama teacher might have entered the children's 'play', in order to challenge the participants, and create a learning experience.

Example: The Flintstones

Setting the topic
- *Topic is agreed for the drama ahead of the lesson (teacher or pupil idea), to allow the teacher some thinking and planning time.*
- *The children are involved in adapting the space to create a Stone Age environment (moving furniture, using cloth for a river, tables for caves, etc.).*

Getting started:
- *Teacher (in role as Fred or Wilma Flintstone) greets the assembled group in notional role as fellow cave-dwellers, and helps the children rationalise who would be engaged in what activities, and organising them within the space: 'what job will you be doing today?'. . . 'are you the person who cooks the food – yes or no?'. . . 'who helps you carve the arrows?'. . . etc.*
- *Children in role set about their regular Stone Age activities.*

Deepening their belief and commitment:
- *Teacher-in-role wanders around amongst the children in role as Stone Age folk, questioning them about what they are doing.*
- *Teacher pauses the action momentarily, and helps them stay focused and on task, by encouraging children to question one another about their tasks.*
- *Teacher resumes role, and calls the group together to consolidate a group feeling: ritualistic shared meal or sing-song round the camp fire (also to create atmosphere of peace and tranquillity to contrast with tension of the next scene).*
- *A dinosaur is spotted! (either spontaneously perhaps by one of the children, or else interjected by the teacher-in-role).*

Intervening towards a resolution
- *Teacher-in-role works to challenge the children's assumptions about an easy solution, and steps in, e.g. with 'No way! Not me . . . I'm not going past that dinosaur to get in that helicopter, and in any case, I'm scared of heights. . .'*

- *The teacher watches for the way they respond, and looks to support their initiative, to lead them towards considering the implications of their actions and behaviour. Possible directions may be anticipated by the teacher:*
  1. *The children instruct the inept teacher-in-role how to move past the dinosaur without it noticing (practising tip-toeing and then moving as slowly as possible, freezing if an assistant-in-role as the dinosaur turns round).*
  2. *Alternatively, the children reconsider an alternative escape from the situation, for example, how to hide from the dinosaur. Possibilities might include playing a glorified 'Musical Statues' game with a teacher-in-role as dinosaur snooping around the children keeping as still as possible; alternatively, the children may hide in a cave in the hillside, created by a human tunnel on their hands and knees.*
  3. *Alternatively, they cooperate and negotiate with one another to trap and capture the dinosaur . . . Find the owner of the dinosaur (Fred or Wilma Flintstone, played by teacher in role) and persuade him or her to help.*
  4. *. . . Or they explore some other solution suggested by the group.*

Without actually dismissing their creative initiative regarding the helicopter, in the above example, the teacher finds a way to challenge the appropriateness of the children's 'quick fix' solution. Here, at the point where the children were beginning to cruise with the narrative, the quick-witted teacher spotted a possible learning area in the unfolding narrative – a shared meaning to do with a universal issue and theme relating to human experience: the notion that a potentially dangerous animal has to be treated thoughtfully and with respect in order to keep everyone safe. The teacher then gave shape to the drama 'on the hoof', and supported the children in thinking through a more viable alternative strategy, leading eventually to a satisfactory resolution, even if it proved problematic along the way – that is all part of the learning.

Perhaps the solution turns out to be *unsatisfactory* – out of role, afterwards, the children could reflect on what was unsuccessful, and with hindsight, what might have been more effective. The children would be emotionally protected from 'failure' through the use of role, in the knowledge that it was not they who had been unsuccessful, it was the people they were pretending to be – even if their role was only vestigial ('friends of Fred or Wilma Flintstone'). Crucially too, the teacher would encourage the children afterwards, out of role, to extrapolate and generalise learning from the drama, to consider implications for dealing with a situation of similar danger in the real world. (Maybe not with an actual dinosaur, but perhaps an angry-looking dog!).

Drama offers children opportunities to experiment with different ways of engaging with others, and to discover the consequences of their actions and behaviour in safety, one-step-removed. This is the power of drama as a learning medium: constructing contexts for learning, especially (and crucially for children with autism) if the participants are offered the chance to reflect on the experience out of role, and to make connections from the drama to the real world. The physical nature of some of the developments in the above drama, and the intrinsic co-operation and negotiation required, may also incidentally prompt children (even those with autism) to engage in *social play* with one another: a crucial reason to interact, as a means to achieving a desired outcome.

In the above drama, the children were also required to solve a daily problem of living (albeit in an analogous context), and discovered how certain people may respond to particular actions or utterances. Unless children are presented with opportunities to develop their personal powers and genuinely influence others, then their effectiveness in real-life social situations will be severely impaired (Harris 1994; Peter 2000a). The QCA (2001b) similarly recognises the value of drama: 'Drama provides a rich and motivating stimulus to develop a wide range of speaking and listening skills in novel, exciting and real-life situations, including involvement in the community' (p. 6).

But is this kind of drama really possible with children with autism? How could they be enabled to engage meaningfully in the kind of drama described above? The above example may be within the capability of certain children with autism, and could be accessed by others with some modification of the drama conventions used. As already demonstrated, children with autism may have latent ability to engage in drama, and may show interest in social engagement in particular contexts, but for a range of reasons tend not to demonstrate this in their own spontaneous free play:

- some may need to learn about symbolism;
- others may have a grasp of symbolism, but find it difficult to generate and sustain a narrative;
- *all* will experience difficulties, to a greater or lesser degree, with the social skills required for effective group work.

Drama is a group experience, and depends on developing shared meanings and understandings. What is required is a developmental approach to drama for both teacher and children, where all participants may 'gain a handle' and understand the essential elements of make-believe, while at the same time, also exploring some aspect of human experience. But how?

A drama continuum

There is a common misconception that planning drama contradicts what drama ought to be about. The teacher actually has a *range of options* on planning. Skilled, experienced drama teachers, for the sake of their own professional development, will aim eventually to work towards pulling back the extent to which a lesson is pre-planned. They will look to be able to hand over 'ownership' to the children from the outset (the 'what shall we do drama about today?' approach), with the ultimate responsibility of shaping the lesson 'on the hoof' to ensure a worthwhile learning experience. That is not to say that a pre-planned lesson is inferior – far from it! Especially with challenging groups – children with autism being a case in point – it is always the teacher's ultimate responsibility to ensure a worthwhile learning experience.

The point is, that any drama lesson will always be a combination of teacher input and child input, which will affect the extent to which the drama may be pre-planned ahead of the lesson. The ratio will depend on:

- the teacher's own confidence and experience;
- the experience and confidence of the group and the teacher's perception of their need for a new challenge;
- the particular ideas the teacher wants to explore or experiences he or she wants the group to have.

For the teacher working with children with autism, the difficulty in developing drama is their relative inability to pick up the nugget of an idea, and to spontaneously elaborate, extend, develop or embroider it. It is remarkable how other children, even those with severe learning difficulties, will often inject a problem or challenge to be solved into their play. In fact, from the mainstream drama teacher's point of view, that can often be the flip side of the coin: how do you decide from the many ideas coming at you, which one will be the one to go with and explore? Teachers working with children with autism, however, may experience the opposite problem: limited relevant responses, or else highly idiosyncratic, inflexible suggestions; either way, they will be under considerable pressure to carry the lesson and hold together the emerging fragile fiction. Novice drama teachers will find themselves not only teaching the children about how drama works while doing it, but also at the same time, needing to learn for themselves how to manipulate, control and structure the drama from within!

A developmental approach to drama may offer a structured framework whereby boundaries may be gradually broadened for the benefit of both teacher and children, yet which may offer plenty of scope within which participants may learn to make appropriate choices and creative decisions within clear parameters. A useful approach to developing drama with children with autism has proved to be that proposed in *Drama for All* (Peter 1994) and *Making Drama Special* (Peter 1995). This drama continuum can be usefully mapped onto the developmental approach to play described in the previous chapter (see Figure 4.1).

While the focus of any drama lesson should always be on the content (ideas, attitudes and issues to be explored), at a subsidiary level, there should always be a

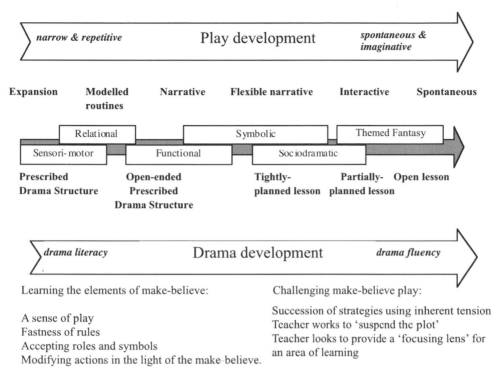

Figure 4.1 A play/drama continuum

teaching aim of advancing children's ability to work within the art form of drama. Bolton (1979) identifies this as being concerned with acquiring the basic drama/theatre skills of:

- selecting a focus;
- injecting tension;
- creating meaningful symbols.

For children with autism at earlier stages of their understanding of make-believe (sensori-motor, relational or functional levels of observed play), learning about the drama form will necessarily be concerned with understanding the 'language of drama' (Peter 1994).

Learning the language of drama

At the core of the approach is a pivotal framework termed a 'Prescribed Drama Structure' (PDS). This somewhat clumsy title is given to a ritualised activity that resembles a game, with a clearly defined beginning-middle-end. Based on an original formulation devised by John Taylor (1984), it enables participants to learn the language of drama – to understand the essential elements of make-believe:

- *a sense of play* (emerging awareness of make-believe: an 'as if' situation in time and space, with its inherent tension and underlying meaning);
- *the fastness of rules* (everyone to 'play the game' in order to sustain the pretence and 'suspend disbelief');
- *accepting roles and symbols* (taking and playing another, consenting to make-believe 'as if', and substitution of objects to be something else);
- *modifying actions in the light of the make-believe* (adapting one's behaviour in response to the 'as if' drama situation, and interaction/communication with others).

In a sense, a PDS is like a glorified drama game, but differs from typical 'warm up' energisers, in that the make-believe context is crucial, with someone always in a character role (usually a member of staff or other adult, especially at first). Participants are necessarily caught up in the developing fiction – and emerging narrative – right from the outset, rather than having to wait for the magic point where they might be deemed 'ready for drama'. In this way, they may experience the elements of make-believe in the same kind of 'game of theatre' (Bolton 1992), which is possible to foster even in very young children, whether or not they are able to articulate it. When young babies first discover pretence, it is very often through repeatedly throwing a rattle out of their cot. Of course, what they discover, and delight in, is that they can cause their parent or carer to feign annoyance, and can generate the pretence through their repeated action and the adult's predictable response . . . again, and again and again!

Recapturing the essence of this kind of scenario in a PDS will appeal to the tendencies and preferences of children with autism for ritualised obsessive behaviours and for generating predictable responses from adults. Like the baby in the cot, through a PDS children with autism may be offered repeated opportunities in which they may learn to generate and sustain pretence within a secure, familiar structure based on turn taking. In a PDS, the 'game of theatre' is made explicit, to enable participants to learn about the elements of make-believe (the language of drama), while actually engaged in the fictitious context from the very outset: even at the most basic level, role is used, so that participants are necessarily caught up in the make-believe.

The predictable generation of make-believe through using a PDS may become a pivot for expanding and developing more lateral thinking, and for gradually pushing the boundaries as participants become more confident in making and negotiating creative choices and decisions. Because the PDS is carefully structured, children's involvement can be paced and closely monitored. Incidental spin-offs will be training in group work, and increasing confidence of staff and children in negotiating within the make-believe, using drama conventions (especially working in role), handling tension (peaks of anxiety, moments of calm, etc.) and modelling appropriate play responses. As indicated previously, the attitude and commitment of supporting staff will be crucial in generating the appropriate 'as if' atmosphere, with pitches of excitement and calm, moments of tension and suspense. Supporting staff should be fully briefed and familiar with the activity, especially the ditties that help create the ritual framework.

Example: The Three Little Pigs

This drama is pitched at the mid-point along the play continuum described in the previous chapter. It works from the basis of a familiar narrative, but follows a parallel course: the soap opera genre – 'meanwhile, elsewhere . . . '. It offers scope to be modified or extended for children at earlier or more advanced stages of their understanding and use of play, but at the same time enables them all to access a *shared meaning* as part of a group. This is the aim in drama terms: *to offer constructive means to help Mrs Pig, who needs to clean up her house in time for her three little pigs returning home.* Rather than acting out the story in the form of the predictable sequence (as in Play Structure 3, page 136), it challenges the children to hold two storylines in mind: the narrative as known, and this deviation: will the two be reconciled at some point? It retains elements of the predictable however, in the turn-taking format, and can (and should) of course be repeated on more than one occasion – ideally over several sessions; for example linked to regular Literacy Hour work or equivalent (DfEE 1998).

Within the ritualistic, repetitive framework, the teacher would aim to encourage participants to respond more purposefully, and look for indicators of confident engagement both with the tasks within the drama, and with the teacher-in-role and possibly other children or staff caught up within the drama. Also a greater sense of ease with the drama form: understanding and use of the format of the lesson, with responses more appropriate and on task. An awareness of the assessed play potential of children with autism will enable the teacher initially to support them in their observed preferred response, but over subsequent sessions, gradually to challenge their responses within the drama. The drama may thus provide a meaningful context within which the teacher may support the children in discovering an intrinsic reward from using their latent more advanced play strategies. When their play is harnessed as a means to an end, the children may perceive the relevance and experience their actions as having a direct consequence in achieving a satisfying outcome.

Objectives
- To adapt behaviour ('suspend disbelief') in notional, collective role (themselves caught up in a fiction) in response to an adult in role.
- To identify and select items associated with particular household tasks and use appropriately.

- To show involvement in group activity, taking turns and joining in without protest (individual targets).

Resources
- A set of items associated with household chores (mop, broom, duster, washing up bowl, scourer sponge, plates and tea towel, dustpan and brush, J-cloth, saucepan and wooden spoon, mixing bowl and tablespoon).
- Photographs or corresponding pictorial images of the above items mounted on a portable felt board.
- Masking tape.
- Apron or pinafore (for teacher-in-role as Mrs Pig).

Introduction (establishing the topic)
- Sit the group on chairs in one corner (or else have them sitting on the floor, securely positioned against the classroom wall with supporting staff alongside or behind as necessary).
- Teacher reads the traditional story of The Three Little Pigs, using a picture storybook and corresponding objects of reference to bring the story to life (e.g. pig dolls or puppets, wolf puppet, models of the three houses – straw, sticks and bricks). Teacher then involves the group in a re-telling of the story, using the items to sequence the familiar narrative.
- Teacher involves the group in creating the drama space: moving furniture away, and creating the façade of Mrs Pig's house, eliciting suggestions from the group, using masking tape outlines to position windows and the door on a room-divider screen (or upturned tables).
- Teacher shows the group Mrs Pig's apron, and explains that when she or he puts this on, she or he will be pretending to be Mrs Pig (show the group the corresponding image of Mrs Pig at the opening of the story, as she waves off her little pigs).

Starting the drama
- Teacher puts on Mrs Pig's apron in full view of the class, then enters the drama space, emerging from behind the façade of the house, to greet the group in role as Mrs Pig, and thanks them for coming to her house.
- Mrs Pig shows the group the household items in turn, encourages the group to name them accordingly and to identify their functional use; similarly, their corresponding photograph or picture on the felt board – she explains that this is to remind her of the jobs she has to do that day.

Deepening (development and exploration)
- Mrs Pig signals through her role that she is fed up, adopting a suitable pose and

facial expression (supporting staff in role alongside the children having been briefed to draw this to the children's attention).

- In role still as Mrs Pig, teacher-in-role explains that she is fed up because she always has so much work to do . . . Pause to allow sufficient time for the children to make connections. If this is unforthcoming (quite likely children with autism may have difficulty working out implications from the situational clues provided), then teacher-in-role could offer a solution to the situation: please could the children help with her jobs.

- Each child in turn is invited to choose a task from the selection of photographs or pictures on the felt board (pointing, signing or verbalising). This could be framed with a ditty:

> Which job will [Ross] choose, [Ross] choose, [Ross] choose
> Which job will [Ross] choose, to help Mrs Pig?

- The child then has to remain faithful to his or her choice and find the corresponding real items from the selection available on a nearby table top. The child then is required to improvise the associated task, using the chosen item appropriately. As the child works, everyone is to say, sing, chant or rap:

> [Sweeping up] for Mrs Pig,
> Mrs Pig, Mrs Pig,
> [Sweeping up] for Mrs Pig,
> [Ross] gets it done.

- As jobs are completed, the corresponding picture can be turned over or removed. In this way, the activity can be pitched so that particular children are targeted according to their ability to make a choice, maybe one of the first to have a turn from a wider range, or towards the end from a more limited range.

- As each child completes his or her chosen task to the rousing accompaniment, Mrs Pig's facial expression should change markedly to a beaming smile (explicitly pointed out to the group), before lapsing again to a fed up pose as she remembers what else needs to be done.

- When everyone has had a turn, Mrs Pig thanks the group, and invites them back another time (same time next week?)

Reflection

- Teacher then stops the drama and removes Mrs Pig's apron, talking through and explaining to the group what is happening. The group should be involved in returning the classroom to its previous state.

- Out of role, the teacher then encourages the children to make connections between the drama and the real world (for example, what jobs need to be done at home to keep the house clean and tidy? How could they help their Mum, Dad or carer, and so cheer them up?).

Suggestions
The above activity should be differentiated according to the play potential of the participants as assessed in structured play situations. Initially, however, the first time the activity is run, it is preferable for participants to consolidate their preferred free play behaviour, and to focus on the group experience: the novelty of the activity is likely to militate against attending to the complexity of potential challenges.

Level 1 – expansion:
Andrew to be prompted by member of staff alongside as necessary, directing his attention and encouraging him to choose, pick up and engage in *sensori-motor* exploration of the corresponding item; through repeated running of the activity, aim to increase Andrew's tolerance of guidance and greater focusing of attention, and more appropriate *relational* play with the items.

Level 2 – modelled routines:
Ellie to select familiar items initially and use appropriately in *relational* play (for example, picking up a spoon and taking to her mouth); through repeated running of the activity, aim to increase Ellie's *functional* play with other items (for example, imitating a supporting member of staff using the spoon to pretend to stir food in the saucepan).

Level 3 – narrative:
Ross to engage initially in appropriate *functional* play with his chosen items (for example, cleaning the floor with the mop); through repeated running of the activity, aim to encourage Ross to select other items and extend and explore alternative *functional* ways of using them (for example, mopping the floor, then plunging the mop in the bucket and squeezing it out).

Level 4 – flexible narrative:
Sophie to demonstrate a range of *functional* activities with chosen items from the outset; through repeated running of the activity, aim to consolidate this through introducing new household tasks and associated items for her to use. Alternatively, substitute similar items from previous weeks (for example, a different type of mop, a washing up brush rather than scourer sponge, etc.), which she is required to use functionally as before.

Level 5 – interactive:
William to engage initially in established *functional* play with a supporting member of staff, another child or Mrs Pig herself (for example, sweeping up, one using the

dustpan, the other the brush; alternatively, washing up with someone else drying). Through repeated running of the activity, introduce materials that may be used *symbolically* within chosen tasks (for example, cotton wool for mashed potato, plasticine rolls for sausages, for William to prepare 'bangers and mash' supper for the three little pigs).

Level 6 – spontaneous:
Jamie to think up and carry out a task not on the board (for example, the ironing) and to mime the activity, possibly using another item *symbolically* (for example, table top to represent the ironing board); through repeated running of the activity, Jamie to be encouraged to combine and sequence different tasks, and to select from a range of available found sources to create new *symbolic* transformations.

Prescribed Drama Structures: effective teaching for children with autism

Psychological research has evidenced how children at early stages of learning are particularly sensitive to rhyme, rhythm and repetition in language (Chukovsky 1963; Bryant and Bradley 1985); also how the motive for early turn-taking exchanges between a parent or carer and the child seems to be mutual enjoyment from human interaction for its own sake (Vygotsky 1978). Bruner (1975b) similarly refers to 'joint actions formats': the creation by parents and carers of simplified and stereotyped sequences of actions with objects and an ebb and flow of tension that are repeated over and over, so that the young child can learn that these are potent focus points of shared meanings.

The young child typically will learn to imitate play responses within the predictable framework, so that a mutual dialogue develops between adult and child, where both may lead or respond. The introduction of an unpredictable element, however small, can provide a reason to comment and challenge the child's existing frame of reference. The inclusion of these elements in a Prescribed Drama Structure (PDS) therefore, not only promotes the communication skills of children with autism, but also captures any wandering attention and brings them back to the shared focus, through the intrinsic pleasure of the experience. A Prescribed Drama Structure such as that illustrated above harnesses several teaching strategies that are known to be particularly successful for children with autism (see Figure 4.2).

Firstly, boundaries around the make-believe are tight, which will enable beginners in drama to feel *secure*: the ritual, turn-taking format enables children to grasp how the generation of make-believe is contained within the familiar chants, song or rhyme; choices and decisions are clear-cut, and do not require imaginative leaps into the realm of the unpredictable. The children are not required to 'act' as such (in the sense of taking the part of a particular character), but simply to be

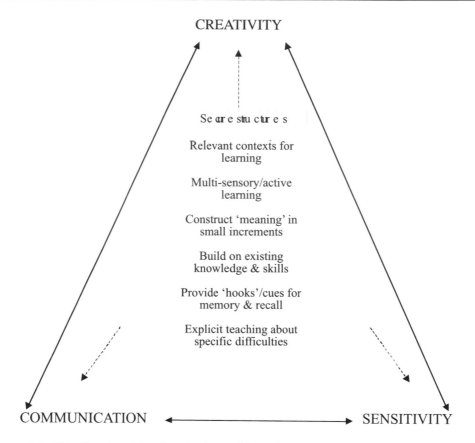

Figure 4.2 Effective teaching for children with autism

themselves caught up in an experience. This also enables them to focus on the content of the drama, their feeling responses and those of others, without the additional complexity of characterisation.

In a PDS, the drama is also built up in very *small increments*, painstakingly constructed with the children's involvement. 'What would you do if . . .' is brought into the here-and-now, thus circumventing complex language constructions. The make-believe is made very explicit and clearly framed (when it is starting and stopping, supported by use of simple props): the intention is to help the children into the symbolism, not delude them by drifting gradually and imperceptibly into it. For example, talking the children through the transformation of their regular classroom equipment (the tables to become the front of a house) and using items flexibly, so that they may accept and grasp the symbolic significance of this.

The children are required in a PDS to *build on their existing knowledge and resources* to help resolve a situation (in this case, to cheer up Mrs Pig by helping her with her jobs), and to draw on their *practical skills* in tasks that are directly within their experience and capabilities (they are all likely to have witnessed parents and carers involved in housework, and may well have participated in such tasks). This is crucially important for children with autism, who may struggle to project into a fantasy situation and extrapolate their resourcefulness beyond their everyday life experiences. Talking about the drama afterwards ('is there a job you could do at home to help?') will further enable them to see the *relevance*. Children with autism are likely to become uninterested and disaffected if they cannot immediately see the point of an activity; once lost, it can be very difficult to redirect them, owing to their overriding tendency towards rigidity of thought and single focused attention.

A PDS such as that illustrated above, includes strategies that also take account of the interrelatedness of the four dimensions of autistic thinking (Powell and Jordan 1997):

- the way information is perceived;
- the way in which the world is experienced;
- the way in which information is coded, stored and retrieved in memory;
- the role of emotion as a context in which those processes may or may not operate.

The *multi-sensory*, 'hands on' approach in a PDS, using a range of tactile, visual and auditory cues, offers a range of levels for the participants to access the shared meaning and the group experience, according to their preferred sensory mode and idiosyncratic interpretation of sensory information (Powell and Jordan 1997). This will maximise the chance of an individual engaging with the experience: while children with autism may be aware at one level that things are happening, they are not always aware that those things are happening to them. The immediacy of the drama prompts them to become aware of their own reactions (it is 'live' and self-affirming), and also those of others (a receptive state in which to engage with other people).

Multi-sensory approaches in a PDS with children with autism will also help redress the impaired sense of an 'experiencing self' (Powell and Jordan 1997) – themselves caught up in an experience – and consequent difficulty with autobiographical memory and recall of events in which they have been personally involved. It is unclear to what extent perceptual irregularities in children with autism create conceptual problems, or whether it is difficulties with conceptual understanding (the evaluation of meaning and significance and its relationship with cognition, as indicated above) that cause difficulties in perception (Powell and Jordan 1997). Either way, drama can help address both elements of this transactional relationship between concept and percept.

Props are used within the drama as *visual hooks* – they provide a means for children with short attention spans to come and go, returning each time to the unfolding narrative without 'losing the plot', as this is made explicit through the arrangement of pictorial cues and corresponding items themselves. The props may also be used afterwards, outside the drama, as *objects of reference* to support memory and recall of the experience: this will be triggered by their appearance, and will thus enable children with autism to utilise their sense of self and memories attached to this. Props are very helpful for indicating clearly the use of role; they need to be simple and easily removable (a hat, jacket, walking stick or apron as in the above PDS), in order to pause the drama momentarily to check everyone is 'with it', or to deal with any management issues that cannot be addressed within the drama.

However, it is important not to overwork the use of teacher-in-role, as the emerging fiction is very fragile, and children may easily become confused and literally 'lose the plot'. Hamming up the character and going over the top with elaborate costume may distract the children from what is being signalled through the role. Children with autism are often intrigued by a familiar adult (teacher or supporting member of staff in role) playing a character that is somewhat detached from reality, in the same way that they often find it less threatening to relate to puppets. For the same reason, mask work is often a successful medium with children with autism. In a PDS however, clear use of facial expression is being advocated, in order through use of role, to *teach explicitly* about changes in emotional state – an area where children with autism are fundamentally challenged, yet which drama is able to target directly.

In drama, the children are involved in *active learning* par excellence – drama is energising and stimulating, so that the event is more likely to be remembered: drama will evoke emotional arousal in the mid-brain and therefore contribute to cortical operations of thinking and problem-solving (Iveson 1996). Drama directly targets, therefore, those parts of the brain that appear damaged in children with autism (Damasio and Maurer 1978). Through drama, it is possible not only to stimulate an emotional reaction, but also directly to teach children with autism about emotions – how to evaluate their own responses and imbue situations with personal meaning, and so also learn to read the reactions of others and develop empathy. Such emotionally salient experiences in drama make ripe contexts for learning: making children with autism aware of how they are feeling about what they are doing, and also capitalising on their natural involvement and engagement to maximise other learning opportunities (to be explored more fully in Chapters 5 and 6).

Developing drama

A PDS gradually enables children with autism to learn to innovate and take initiative confidently and relevantly, through clearly defined choices within a fixed structure. In devising a PDS, teachers need to consider the kind of response anticipated from individual children: their preferred free play behaviour, and their assessed potential within a structured play situation, as well as their level of social play (see previous chapter). A PDS should have the following features (Peter 1994):

- an element of *make-believe*, with everyone caught up in the fiction from the outset;
- a *rule-based* format, maybe with the idea of some sanction;
- an element of *tension*, involving feelings of anticipation of some peak of excitement or impending disaster, and elements of fear or threat in a safe situation;
- a *ritual* element, maybe controlled by music, a rhythm, rhyme or chant, to reinforce commitment to the activity;
- *interaction* with others, both in and out of role, and an opportunity to have influence and create impact;
- *active participation* in tasks with immediate cause–effect consequences of action and behaviour;
- a *communal* experience, involving all staff and pupils, with extraneous distractions minimised as far as possible;
- some aspect of *cross-curricular* learning included, or an aspect of learning from core and foundation subjects.

Children may achieve progress by:

- adapting the same PDS for a new play challenge (as above);
- proceeding to a different PDS, but at the same level of play challenge;
- proceeding to a new PDS at their higher level of potential play;
- proceeding to an open-ended PDS with an unexpected outcome that involves a problem to be resolved.

It is important for the teacher to retain an open mental set, in order not to dominate the activity, and to encourage participants' creativity in ways illustrated above. A PDS may be used flexibly as a pivot activity: a framework in which to develop increasingly challenging make-believe contexts. It can be elaborated (for example, extending the interaction demands from participants), and may be opened up through introducing an unexpected problem or dilemma. In this way the 'lid is taken off', so that the drama becomes *open-ended* with an unexpected outcome in the eyes of the pupils, even if, covertly, the teacher may have anticipated (but not totally predicted!) a few possible directions the course of events might take.

For example, in the above drama, perhaps one day Mrs Pig does not emerge from her house – what could be the matter? Is she ill? Hurt? In need of their help somehow? Various pieces of medical equipment could be made available (stethoscopes, eye-patches, empty plastic bottles of medicine and tablets, teaspoons, slings, splints, so that the children can administer a range of treatments to the ailing Mrs Pig. The children should be encouraged to engage with the activity and respond to specific requests for attention, e.g. 'Ooow . . . my foot hurts. Oh dear, I'm feeling dizzy. . . '. They should be encouraged to interact both with Mrs Pig (teacher-in-role) and with one another – maybe cooperate to make her a cup of tea.

As the teacher gains confidence in handling drama, so 'taking the lid off' a PDS is a crude, unpressured way to ease into open-ended drama: essentially by setting up a 'game' which then involves some kind of free negotiation in its outcome. In the above example, the teacher would go with the group's desired and agreed direction, to resolve the particular situation, and to lead them to see directly the implications of their suggestions both within the drama and afterwards out of role (for example, thinking how they could help someone in a similar situation in real life). In this way, the teacher gives shape to the children's *symbolic play* in order to address a particular area of learning, so that they confront their existing ideas, and are led to gain insights into themselves and others.

Once the teacher is comfortable with the approach, and the participants are engaging freely within the make-believe and with one another, so it will be appropriate to plan for more open-ended drama more rigorously, and explore a wider range of drama conventions at the teacher's disposal, for giving shape to an unfolding narrative. This will be considered in the following chapter, linked to focused planned learning opportunities across the curriculum.

CHAPTER 5

Learning *through* Drama: play as a learning medium

The extent to which any drama lesson is pre-planned will depend on the teacher's agenda and the kind of learning experiences he or she wishes the class to have. Drama's subject matter essentially is *human experience,* aspects of which are explored and illuminated as characters get to grips with some problem to be solved or dilemma to be faced. Drama offers opportunities for participants to reflect on why people think and behave as they do. It also offers the chance to experiment with different ways of engaging with others and to discover the consequences of their actions and behaviour. This happens in the safety of the make-believe, enabling children to learn from successes and mistakes made by their fictitious roles. This chapter looks in depth at the drama process, and the planning necessary for more open-ended drama with children with autism, which aims to *challenge and extend their symbolic play.*

The notion of *learning through drama* is also explored in relation to children with autism. Possibilities are considered for challenging and extending their play to explore areas of learning across the curriculum. In many children with autism, their play may remain latent or be assessed as quite limited in free-play situations, although as indicated earlier, structured play situations (including drama) may reveal their potential. Chapter 4 illustrated the value of drama to children with autism, *including* those at early stages of learning. Not only can drama harness successful strategies that take account of the autistic way of thinking, but also offer emotionally charged contexts for learning. This chapter will explore further the opportunities in drama for teachers to capitalise on their engagement with the experience, and how drama can directly address the 'triad of impairments' (Wing 1996) experienced by children with autism: difficulties with rigidity of thought, communication and social interaction.

The drama process

In more open-ended drama work, the intention is that there will always be a distinct phase (although this may be of varying length), where participants are required to negotiate freely within the make-believe towards achieving collectively a particular outcome to a situation. This phase may be of varying lengths. It will be the teacher's responsibility to give shape to this *intervention/resolution phase* in process, and to enable the children afterwards to reflect on the area of learning explored. It may well be that the teacher has anticipated certain directions for the drama. The important thing however, is that the teacher's mental set should remain open to possibilities and the initiatives of the group, and that an original plan may need to be abandoned at any stage of the lesson if a more viable learning area emerges.

This can feel like a daunting challenge for the teacher of children with autism! Does this mean that the teacher is always honour-bound to follow the direction of a particular child? How can the teacher reconcile the wishes – or learning needs – of an individual with those of the group? How can the teacher (or well-intentioned supporting staff) avoid hi-jacking the course of action? How can children with autism be helped to engage with the significance of an event in the unfolding drama? How can the teacher enable a group with such highly idiosyncratic children to stay focused? Is it possible to embrace the unpredictability of children with autism and yet sustain the unfolding tension and group dynamic?

These are very real questions, and will be considered in due course. However, initially, it is necessary to understand how the *drama process* works. Assuming that teachers are confident in leading Prescribed Drama Structures (PDS), they will be well versed in the 'language of drama':

- handling dramatic tension (moments of excitement, calm, suspense, etc.);
- modelling appropriate play responses (ensuring cooperation and consensus to 'play the game', establishing adequate management control and boundaries);
- negotiating in role with the children and supporting staff (empowering and enabling the children through effective questioning and responding flexibly to developments);
- adapting their own behaviour in the light of the make-believe (signalling information, directions or instructions confidently in role).

It was suggested in Chapter 4 that teachers could begin to ease themselves into more open-ended drama work by opening up a PDS, injecting a 'problem' into the situation, so that it has an unexpected outcome in the eyes of the children. The teacher would nevertheless have anticipated fairly safely some likely directions, and would have watched for which way the group wished to go, then endeavoured to slow the drama down to make them work at resolving the situation. The teacher would have supported the group towards negotiating within the make-believe and led the group through an improvised outcome to the drama: he or she would have identified potential areas of learning, and handled inherent tension in the situation to explore one avenue of development in process. Essentially it is this ability that teachers need in order to teach open-ended drama competently: sharpening negotiation skills, and leading the children to a focus – a learning experience – by giving shape to their symbolic play using a range of drama and theatre conventions (more of those later, in Chapter 6).

A competent drama teacher will approach planning a lesson with a more rigorous awareness of the *drama process* (see Figure 5.1), and a clear sense of intention for the various stages of the drama. Any drama, at whatever level of sophistication, has this same underlying structure; it is the surface organisation and the use of drama and theatre conventions that will vary. In order to respond flexibly and sensitively to meet the needs of the group, teachers will need to expand their repertoire of drama knowledge and strategies. The following chapter identifies certain 'fail safe' drama conventions that can be particularly effective when working with children with autism. At first it may be a case of planning these rationally and methodically, but as teachers become more practised, so they may be able to call upon these more automatically and intuitively to respond spontaneously to a development in the drama in process.

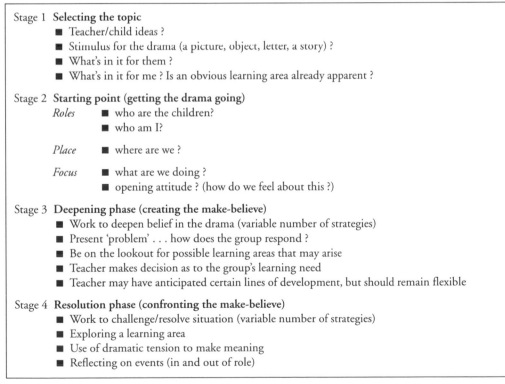

Stage 1   **Selecting the topic**
- Teacher/child ideas ?
- Stimulus for the drama (a picture, object, letter, a story) ?
- What's in it for them ?
- What's in it for me ? Is an obvious learning area already apparent ?

Stage 2   **Starting point (getting the drama going)**
Roles   who are the children?
              who am I?

Place   where are we ?

Focus   what are we doing ?
              opening attitude ? (how do we feel about this ?)

Stage 3   **Deepening phase (creating the make-believe)**
- Work to deepen belief in the drama (variable number of strategies)
- Present 'problem' . . . how does the group respond ?
- Be on the lookout for possible learning areas that may arise
- Teacher makes decision as to the group's learning need
- Teacher may have anticipated certain lines of development, but should remain flexible

Stage 4   **Resolution phase (confronting the make-believe)**
- Work to challenge/resolve situation (variable number of strategies)
- Exploring a learning area
- Use of dramatic tension to make meaning
- Reflecting on events (in and out of role)

Figure 5.1 The drama process

When first venturing into more systematic planning for open-ended drama, it may be more viable to plan for a clear learning area, where the teacher has in mind a specific issue for the group to explore (see Figure 5.2 – model A). The teacher would then plan a flexible route (building in plenty of opportunities for creative initiatives) to a particular point where that focus can then be tackled. For example, a problem may be *introduced* (planned by the teacher) that causes the participants to be put on their mettle, and prompts them to think through possible solutions to the situation (see the example of 'Monet's garden' below). These solutions should be well within the abilities of the group to use their resourcefulness towards achieving a satisfactory outcome. The teacher would call upon different drama strategies and conventions in order to structure contexts in which the participants can work towards a resolution, and gradually be brought to a shift in their thinking according to their reactions and responses.

In order to progress their own professional development, drama teachers will need to be prepared to limit the extent to which an open-ended drama lesson is pre-planned. For example: have a topic in mind, an opening and one or two strategies for deepening the participants' belief in the drama (see Figure 5.2 – model B). However, having set up the drama and being confident that the children are 'running with it', the teacher may be alert to a possible learning area *emerging* (as in the Flintstones drama described above, where the children were on the point of cruising over the issue of dealing responsibly with a dangerous animal). It is a case of the teacher being prepared to work more 'at risk' and trusting to the children's initiatives, confident that certain fail-safe drama strategies (see Chapter 6) may usefully support children (especially those with autism) in getting to grips with the issue in focus.

In time – and with practice (it's a steep learning curve, where you learn fast through mistakes!) – the teacher may be able to negotiate all decisions for the drama with the group from the outset (see Figure 5.2 – model C). This is a very challenging – and potentially exposing – way of teaching, and really requires a high level of expertise to ensure that the children will be offered a worthwhile learning experience. However, for the sake of completeness to the model, it is offered here as the logical extension for professional development in drama teaching. As already indicated, the additional pressures that children with autism can place on the drama teacher are considerable and should not be underestimated. Perhaps it is more viable for the aspiring drama teacher to focus instead on developing greater thoroughness and differentiation in planning:

- for the various areas of learning across the curriculum that may be addressed within any one lesson (learning *through* drama);
- for individual progress in understanding and using increasingly challenging drama and theatre conventions (learning *in* drama);

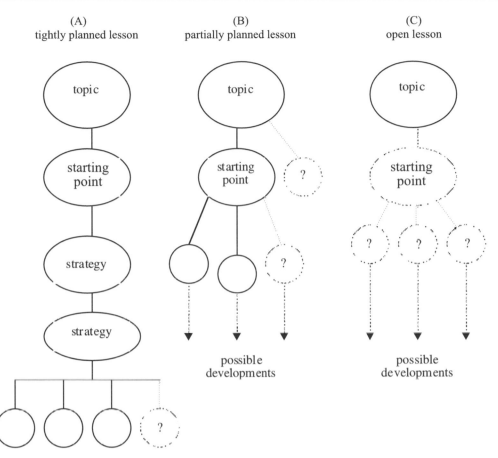

Figure 5.2 Models for open-ended drama

- for progress in understanding and using narrative – creating and exploring script (learning *about* drama).

Learning *in* and *about* drama will be explored more fully in Chapters 6 and 7. The rest of this chapter will focus in depth on learning opportunities *through* drama for children with autism. There follows an example of a drama lesson (adapted from Peter 1996a; and a subsequent reworking in Jordan *et al.* 2001) that illustrates the multi-layered potential of drama as a learning medium. It demonstrates how drama can potentially offer a highly meaningful, synthesising way for children to share, develop and extend their existing knowledge, understanding and skills from a broad base. It also illustrates the potential of drama as an economic approach to curriculum planning!

Example: 'Monet's garden'

This open-ended drama could link with topic work developed from a cross-curricular theme on gardens or the environment; alternatively an art focus or

French theme. The lesson seeks to deepen participants' understanding of the effort required and wider issues involved in the maintenance of a garden – and some of the conflicts resulting from tourism and the effect of cars on the natural peace of a garden. It contextualises a Prescribed Drama Structure (PDS) within a more open-ended drama framework, as a key strategy within the unfolding narrative: rather than as a self-standing drama lesson, the PDS is one drama convention within the teacher's overall plan. By using the PDS as a pivot within the drama, the teacher has the opportunity, when working with an inclusive group, to ensure that the drama is directly pitched at participants' potential level of play development for some, if not all the time.

It will be apparent that the PDS below is a re-working of the example in the previous chapter about Mrs Pig. This is quite deliberate, in order to illustrate how the same *content* can be re-presented, but in a different *context*. This is crucially important for children with autism, who may need to revisit material time and again, yet also need this balanced with fresh contexts in which to explore similar areas of learning. This particular drama offers a more sophisticated content, and would perhaps be appropriate therefore for older participants who may still need to consolidate their understanding of content from earlier stages of learning. As in the previous chapter, the teacher should aim to differentiate the challenges for individual children (refer back to the Mrs Pig PDS for ways to pitch these at differing levels of potential play responses in structured situations). For example:

- modifying the task through supported participation for pupils at *sensori-motor* stages of their play development, with a member of staff alongside to direct attention and prompt as necessary, using pictures as cues to encourage more *relational* play with the items;
- possibly modelling routines for a child at a *relational* level, to encourage more *functional* play with the items;
- extending a child's existing *functional* play by encouraging more flexible use of props and additional *symbolic* use of found sources;
- challenging those able to play *symbolically* further by encouraging free interaction within the make-believe, questioning the children in role and talking with them (for example, about their life as one of the gardeners); also possibly encouraging them to think up and carry out an imaginary task.

Rather than necessarily evolving into a more open-ended drama, the lesson can be stopped when the PDS has run its course. When everyone has had a turn, the teacher-in-role as head gardener thanks the team and asks them back another time (same time next week?). The teacher then stops the drama, clearly signalling that it is finished by taking off the gardening hat, and involving the group in returning the room to its original state. As previously, out of role, participants should be encouraged to make connections between the drama and the real world (for example, 'what jobs need to be done to keep your garden (or the park) looking nice?'). This drama can also be repeated over several sessions, with a view to the children demonstrating increasing engagement, greater awareness and under-standing of the issues being explored and confidence with the dramatic form.

However, even those children who do not yet demonstrate competent symbolic play whether in free or structured play situations, nevertheless may benefit from sharing the 'group buzz' of open-ended drama, albeit at an unarticulated level (the change of atmosphere and the awareness of an 'as if' situation). Their involvement in the open-ended part of the lesson will need to be *modified* through supported participation: the child may be encouraged to focus attention, and expected to show interest, and take some initiative – although this will not necessarily be relevant nor consistently on task. Other children in an inclusive group may need to have their symbolic play *extended*: a child may be expected to express feelings and ideas with understanding and awareness of the mental states of others, and actively encouraged to make constructive suggestions towards resolving the situation in the drama.

Objectives
- To adapt behaviour ('suspend disbelief') to create and sustain collaborative roles, and recall and reflect on the experience (NC ref: English – 4a, 4b, 4c; 11a).
- To consider implications of conflicting interests in improving and sustaining the environment (NC ref: Geography – 5b).
- To explore tasks involved in creating and caring for a garden environment (NC ref: Science – 5c).
- To identify similarities and differences between the lifestyle of Monet and his gardeners and present day lifestyles (NC ref: History – 2b, 6c).
- To consider the Impressionist painting style and use of colour (NC ref: Art – 4a, 4c; 5d).
- To respond appropriately to and use French ways of greeting (NC ref: Modern Foreign Languages – 1a).
- To identify appropriate ways to manage their feelings, and find a constructive means for their voice to be heard (NC ref: PSHE and citizenship – 1a, 1b, 1c; 2a, 2c, 2g).
- To show involvement in group activity, focusing attention, taking turns and joining in appropriately and without protest (targets from Individual Education Plans).

Resources
- A set of objects relating to gardening (trug, trowel, rake, packet of seeds, twine, watering can, etc.).
- Corresponding picture images or photographs of the gardening items, mounted

on a portable board.
- Masking tape.
- Large piece of blue cloth (to represent lily pond).
- Gardening cap (for teacher in role).
- Official peaked cap (for assistant in role or else teacher in switch of role).
- Video – 'Monet's Garden at Giverny'. Plymouth: Two Four Productions Ltd.

Warm up – drama game (optional)
- Sit the group on chairs in a corner of the room, and play 'pass the hot potato' energising game: small sack containing small gardening items to be passed around the circle to an accompanying ditty or chant. The person left holding the sack at the end of the song each time has to pull out an item, name it (if possible) and explain (or show) its use:

  Pass around the garden sack, pass around the garden sack
  Pass around the garden sack until the music STOPS
- Place all the accumulating items together, and put the relevant corresponding pictures on the board, explaining they will be needed for our drama about Monet's garden.

Introduction (establishing the topic)
- Present the group with reproductions of works by the French Impressionist artist, Claude Monet, of his garden at Giverny. Encourage their responses and comments, and provide background information on Monet's impressionist technique (short spontaneous brush strokes) and use of colour (from a limited palette).
- Discuss Monet's lifestyle – show extracts from the video of the interior of Monet's house, and how he created his garden without the help of modern tools and equipment. Emphasise differences between those days and the present.
- Explain that we are going to do a drama about the people who nowadays look after Monet's garden, to keep it nice for the visitors. Discuss the kinds of tasks that are similar to days gone by, and those which are different.
- Show the group an extract of video about Monet's garden, featuring the head gardener talking about some of the tasks his team have to do. Pause the video to draw attention to his hat, and show the group a similar hat which will be used in the drama. (Explain that when you put on the hat later on, you will be pretending to be the head gardener at Giverny.)

Opening (starting the drama)
- Involve the group in creating the drama space: move furniture away, position the lily pond using the blue cloth, use masking tape to delineate pathways, flower borders, etc. according to the group's suggestions.

- Explain they will be the people who look after the garden for the visitors; you will be the head gardener: show them your hat again, and explain that when you next talk to them wearing the hat, you will be pretending to be the head gardener.
- If necessary, re-play a brief extract of the video – or a still frame – to show again to the group the gardener wearing his hat.

Deepening (development and exploration)
- Run a *Prescribed Drama Structure:*
  - Teacher-in-role as head gardener (sporting gardening hat) greets the group (in French – 'bonjour!'), and shakes hands with each in turn as they become the gardening team at Giverny. Teacher shows them the tasks for the day (picture diary on the board), indicating the pile of items for carrying out the tasks, in order to keep the garden nice for the visitors.
  - In turn, the gardeners are to offer to help with a job of their choice from the pictures on the board (pointing, signing or verbalising), and locating the appropriate object to carry out the task.
  - Everyone has a turn with a job (miming the appropriate task using the prop), and each time, the head gardener is extremely grateful.
  - As the child works, everyone is to say, sing, chant or rap:

    > [Doing the weeding] in Monet's garden
    > Monet's garden, Monet's garden
    > [Doing the weeding] in Monet's garden
    > [Jamie] gets it done

- Reconvene a *meeting* of the gardeners, and explain they are about to have a visitor: an important person from the local council (show the peaked cap).
- *Rehearse* in role appropriate ways to greet this official (shaking hands, saying 'bonjour').
- *Ritual:* each gardener in turn shakes hands and greets the official (teacher or assistant in role, wearing an official peaked cap) with 'bonjour'.
- *Teacher or assistant in role* thanks the gardeners for their hard work, and explains that some changes must be made to the garden – there are now so many visitors, that more space must be made for all the cars. This official should make some deliberately provocative suggestions especially relating to the jobs the gardeners have just carried out (for example, digging up the flower beds to make new wide driveways?), all uttered with an ambiguous big smile.

Intervention/resolution (selecting and creating)
- Allow time for the gardeners to make connections and engage them in discussion to help them to think through the implications.

- *'Action replay'* and *'freeze frame'* to highlight the official's expression and analyse possible hidden intentions.
- *Exercise*: Gardeners to make a plan (individually, in pairs or as a small group) of how they think the garden should look – cars or no cars?
- *Meeting*: feedback ideas – reactions? Suggestions? Agree a collective course of action for the whole group.

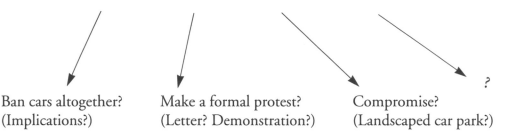

Ban cars altogether?   Make a formal protest?   Compromise?   ?
(Implications?)   (Letter? Demonstration?)   (Landscaped car park?)

Reflection
- Stop the drama, and return the room to its original state.
- Out of role, involve the children in recalling the drama and how they felt about developments, using objects of reference to prompt memory as necessary.
- Lead a discussion over cars and the environment in the real world: should they be banned?

Drama as a learning medium

In the National Curriculum, drama is now a statutory requirement, compared with its original marginalized position when it featured merely as a wall chart, with some passing cross references in subjects across the curriculum (DES 1990). Paradoxically, drama's position has been strengthened within the core subject of English, such that it is now compulsory – the only art in fact to have this status, even though it is not considered a discrete foundation subject as such. Drama directly offers children with autism ways to access the English curriculum, and benefit from opportunities to:

- develop the ability to respond, to listen and to understand;
- interact and communicate effectively with others in a range of social situations;
- make choices, obtain information, question and be actively involved in decision making;
- develop creativity and imagination;
- have access to a wide range of literature to enrich and broaden their experience. (QCA 2001b: 4).

The above drama offers participants specific opportunities to develop their *speaking and listening* skills, and is pitched according to a range of abilities. For example, at

Key Stage 1, the National Curriculum requires children to learn to speak confidently and listen to what others have to say, and at Key Stage 2, to learn to change the way they speak to suit different situations, purposes and audiences (DfEE 1999). When modified for children with autism, this may be interpreted as (based on QCA 2001b):

- communicating by building on previous experiences, and increasingly in a range of contexts and with growing confidence (*repeated opportunity to apply appropriate language to help someone in need*);
- communicating to different listeners and a range of audiences, and an increasing range of functions (*use of role and analogous situations to extend opportunities*);
- working in small groups and in a class, participating and contributing (*opportunities within the drama and out of role, adjusting language accordingly*);
- attending and listening to what others are saying so that they can respond to and recall what has been said, and with a developing vocabulary and in increasingly appropriate ways (*drama providing a shared focus and sense of collaborative purpose*).

The above lesson directly offers opportunities for children with autism to use language to explore their own experiences and imaginary worlds, with drama providing contexts to express their ideas and feelings, and to contribute to situations with different demands (DfEE 1999). Again, the lesson can be modified for an inclusive group of children with autism, to enable meaningful participation at an appropriate level of challenge according to the range of ability. This is explored more fully in Chapter 6, in relation to the dimensions of play at different stages of development.

The 'Monet's garden' example also illustrates how drama may be used to support the development of *literacy* skills in children with autism, capitalising on the opportunity to explore the direct connection between the spoken and written word in a meaningful context. 'The National Curriculum emphasises the importance of interrelating speaking and listening, reading and writing' (QCA 2001b: 5). One possible anticipated outcome could be the formulation of a protest letter to an authority figure, objecting to the development plans for Monet's garden. The most appropriate form of recording should be selected according to the children's needs, whether as a whole class, individually or in small groups; for example, using symbols, text, picture, letter and word stamps, using an adult as scribe, handwriting or computer generated script. The task here directly provides children with autism with a meaningful context in which to develop their composition skills, aimed at a particular purpose and reader. They may work with staff and one another on planning and drafting, with the situation of appealing to authority impelling a need for accurate spelling, punctuation, legible handwriting and neat presentation. After all, a teacher-in-role as a busy official may be legitimately irritated at receiving a scrappy piece of unchecked work!

Drama can offer opportunities for exploring aspects of *subjects across the curriculum*, especially where learning hinges on an understanding of human motivation and causes and consequences of action. The 'Monet's garden' drama links English with aspects of science, history, geography, art, and even modern foreign languages. These may be 'brought to life' through the drama and shared meanings explored. Drama may also provide opportunities for children with autism to generalise and practise learning from core and foundation subjects, and provide a reason and urgency to use practical skills, concepts and factual knowledge (letter formation, for example). These may even be introduced through the drama context, so capitalising on a powerful and memorable active learning opportunity. Drama also provides many situations where social cooperation and negotiation are intrinsically demanded, and where children's spiritual, moral, social and cultural development may be promoted.

Drama can explicitly teach about *empathy and emotions*: it directly targets as its core content aspects of citizenship and the development of children's personal, social and emotional understanding. Engagement in drama happens on a *real* feeling level, even though the context is fictitious. Children with autism can be put directly in touch with their reactions, and encouraged to reflect on them and their consequent actions and behaviour. For example, in the above drama, the teacher in role as head gardener could pointedly describe the feelings of anger he was experiencing, and ask the children (in their roles as gardeners) whether they were feeling the same way. Discussion in role (the meetings) could deliberately focus on ways of dealing appropriately with those feelings: how to channel an urge to shout and scream into a more effective way of raising their view with others (here to authority).

Through drama, participants may be taught how to recognise and respond to their feelings appropriately, and *develop confidence and responsibility in making the most of their abilities*. The 'Monet's garden' example also illustrates the potential of drama to children with autism for *preparing to play an active role as citizens*, explicitly teaching them how to move from a personal world view to a broader perspective, to value and respect differences, and their ability to influence situations. The drama also directly provides contexts both in and out of role to develop and experience a range of relationships, and explicitly teaches how to recognise and understand different types of relationship (for example, coping with formal authority figures). Drama can be instrumental for children with autism *developing good relationships and respecting differences between people*. Specifically, the above drama provides opportunities to (based on QCA 2001c):

- make choices (*both on a concrete level and at a more abstract level of understanding*);
- take part in group activities and discussions (*towards a collaborative purpose*);
- realise that all individuals are important in their own right (*valuing the efforts of menial workers*);

- recognise differences and similarities in people (*lifestyles historically and in the present day, and implications of opposing viewpoints*).

'Keeping tabs' on all the possible developments that may be taking place within such a rich learning context is a daunting task for the teacher, but not insurmountable. Teachers will need to prioritise areas of learning and key assessment opportunities, both for individuals and the group, while nevertheless endeavouring to move forwards on all fronts at the same time, and to be on the alert for surprise developments! It is important however, that children's progress in understanding and using the drama form should not be compromised for the sake of servicing other areas across the curriculum. Additionally of course, teachers should be mindful their own progress and professional development in drama, and seek to evaluate their effectiveness. Appendix C includes consideration of some of the implications for teaching drama, and guidelines for practice.

Drama and 'the triad of impairments'

The QCA (2001b) highlights the following benefits of drama for all children with learning difficulties across the age range, for helping them to develop:

- a sense of self and of their role in different social groups;
- anticipation and recall;
- listening, concentration and attention skills;
- the ability to choose, justify and discriminate between decisions;
- the confidence to experiment and try new ideas where there is no right or wrong answer;
- cooperation, tolerance and willingness to work with others;
- self-discipline and self-confidence and involvement in the community (p. 6).

Through drama experiences, children with autism may be offered opportunities to develop their *thinking skills* and certain *key skills* (QCA 2001a) that will be fundamental to their participation and achievement in all walks of life. Together with thinking skills, the particular key skills of problem solving, communication and working with others relate directly to the 'triad of impairments' (Wing 1996) experienced by children with autism. The implication is that regular drama sessions may result in improvement in the manifesting characteristic features of children with autism, towards a 'triad of competence'.

Thinking and problem solving

Children with autism are fundamentally challenged in their ability to see significance or implications within a situation, and to engage in flexible thinking.

They have particular difficulty with the three combined processes that determine success in thinking (based on QCA 2001a):

- input – obtaining and organising knowledge through sensory awareness and perception to confirm 'what I know' (limited 'sense of self');
- control – thinking through a situation and making actions meaningful (limited ability to evaluate significance);
- output – strategies for using knowledge and solving problems that combine 'what I do' with 'what I know' (tendency to rigidity of thought resulting in poor generalisation, transference of understanding and making connections).

A structured approach to drama can enable children with autism to focus their attention and begin to make selections within clear boundaries, and to see the implications of their choices, so reinforcing their sense of self and their ability to influence others. This occurs in a *social context*, where the participants are encouraged to think through a situation, and explicitly taught the relevance and significance of their responses, and so (literally) discover meaning in action. Through drama children with autism may be explicitly taught ways to think about and generate ideas pertinent to a particular context, with boundaries gradually broadened and carefully paced – refer to the differentiated challenges presented to the children, detailed in the Mrs Pig drama in the previous chapter.

Ways to remember information and access and use their thinking skills will need to be explicitly taught to children with autism, hence the importance of building in opportunities for reflection, both within the drama and afterwards out of role. For example, musing on Mrs Pig's facial expression within the PDS, and reminding them to compare this with a comparable teaching aid photograph of a sad face on the classroom wall. Afterwards (out of role), the children were asked to recall Mrs Pig's expression (perhaps teacher momentarily donning Mrs Pig's apron and adopting the appropriate pose), to offer the children an opportunity to re-use their strategy for working out the meaning of her body language (referring to the classroom photograph again – perhaps spontaneously – with supporting staff prompting as necessary).

Similarly, the Mrs Pig drama illustrates how children with autism may be supported in the retrieval of their knowledge and in developing a sense of resourcefulness within clear boundaries. For example, to make the connection between the happy, cheerful reaction of Mrs Pig and the children's help with her household chores. Afterwards, out of role, the children were encouraged to make a connection with their home setting, and consider noticing if a parent or carer appeared to have the same expression as Mrs Pig when faced with their household chores. In this way, they may be supported in discovering their ability to influence a situation constructively (here, to offer to help).

For children to become independent, they need to be able to solve problems by using knowledge, memory and thinking skills (QCA 2001a). Drama hinges on the notion of a core problem to be solved or a dilemma to consider. In drama it is possible to provide children with autism opportunities to take part in problem-solving activities that motivate, challenge and stimulate their attention. For example, in the Monet's garden example, the participants were required to make a connection that *they* could be in a position to offer help to look after a garden (the PDS), and secondly how they could make their point effectively to people in authority.

Drama requires holding two worlds in mind at the same time: children with autism will be challenged to develop this double-edged facility to 'do it and watch themselves doing it' simultaneously. Developing this state of 'metaxis' (Boal 1981) – mentally holding two perspectives at once – will not only promote their *mental agility*, but also enable them to learn from drama's double-edge. Children with autism will still need support, however, in extrapolating learning from the drama to real life situations: it is crucially important that learning is made explicit in this way, as they may not otherwise see the significance and transfer learning between contexts.

More flexible thinking can be promoted in children with autism by providing opportunities to extend their *imagination*. 'Imagination' is not simply projecting into fantasy situations, such as a walk on the moon or the Australian outback, beyond their actual experience! (It has to be said, however, that TV and video have considerably broadened the horizons of today's children, including those with autism. Current obsessions and interests can all provide a theme or context for drama work.) A more useful way of thinking about 'imagination' may be as the creative use of memory. This immediately enables the teacher to see a facilitating role, in enabling children with autism to access memory.

For example, in the above lesson, clearly the children with autism would not have had direct experience of gardening at Giverny. Nevertheless, using video would have enabled them to bridge the gap, and also recalled tasks that may be within their experience. Appealing to their cognitive strengths – supporting recall through providing objects of reference and visual cues differentiated according to their level of understanding, and providing clear boundaries within which to make a choice or decision – enabled them to communicate a *creative* initiative according to their respective level of development.

Communication

It is crucial that the level of language throughout the lesson is pitched according to the ability of the participants and their level of *symbolic development*. For children with autism, this will mean supporting the spoken word through signing systems and/or objects of reference. These may need to be real objects, toys, small world objects, photographs, picture material, rebus symbols, etc., according to an individual child's level of conceptual understanding. It may also mean using a range of augmentative communication strategies when working with a group with diverse needs.

Drama can actually be instrumental in promoting symbolic development if real objects and props are gradually replaced by more representational and abstract imagery, working towards the unsupported spoken or written word. Likewise, the same prop may be used flexibly for a variety of representational functions: for example, a table to be a cave, an ironing board or a bed. In the Mrs Pig PDS in the previous chapter, the children witnessed tables being upturned to create the façade for a house. They also saw their regular classroom cleaning items (mop, broom, etc.) acquiring a new meaning within the fictitious drama context. A further development might be to replace the real items with playhouse items or makeshift props from found sources, and ultimately to mime activities without the use of any props.

It is important that drama is experienced as stimulating, motivating, challenging and fun, so that children with autism needing to recapture early *pre-verbal foundations* may discover that communication is fun and brings results (Aherne *et al.* 1990). Both the Prescribed Drama Structure in Chapter 4 and the lesson described above illustrate ways in which these foundations may be experienced, as identified by McLean and Snyder-McLean (1985). Participants are provided with:

- opportunities where their communicative attempts are valued;
- a reason to communicate;
- opportunities to make real choices;
- the genuine option of refusing to take part;
- reasons to comment through inclusion of unpredictable elements;
- opportunities to solve a problem to help get out of a fix, however crude;
- interactive, turn-taking activities;
- opportunities to explore different ways of communicating in an alternative role and for varying purposes.

Ultimately, effective communication involves the integration of:

- body movements (body language, facial expression, pointing);
- gestures and visual skills ('reading people');
- communication aids, including objects of reference, photographs, pictures, symbols;
- listening (distinguishing and focusing on relevant sounds from the environment, discriminating and transferring meaning between different forms of human interaction);
- vocalisation and speech (expressing oneself for a range of different functions and

in different contexts and for different audiences).(Based on Edwards 1999; QCA 2001b.)

Drama encourages children with autism of all abilities to express their likes, dislikes, feelings, emotions and preferences. Both in the Mrs Pig and Monet's garden dramas, their vocalisation is actively sought, whether spontaneous or imitative, and they are offered a range of possibilities for communicating through actions and gestures as well as the spoken word, supported with objects of reference and pictorial visual cues as necessary. The ability to attend, listen and discriminate between contrasting stimuli is fundamental for the development of speaking and listening skills in children with autism, given their difficulty in prioritising incoming sensory information. The Mrs Pig PDS illustrates how drama can promote their ability to:

- *listen and develop auditory memory*, for example, responding to sounds in the environment or to the cessation of sound (the familiar ditty and quiet in between), attending to adult imitation of their own sounds (staff mirroring the children's spontaneous utterances to reinforce awareness of their emotional reaction to the drama experience), responding to their own name (Mrs Pig inviting them to help her each in turn), imitation and turn-taking activities (carrying out a household task, modelled by staff in role as necessary), responding appropriately to specific sounds, words and phrases (ritualised utterances couched within the ditty) and exploring language in different contexts (using appropriate social graces within the analogous situation of a guest's house).

- *maintain and develop concentration*, for example, focusing on an activity (the intriguing spectacle of their teacher and everyday classroom equipment in other guises), tracking a sound or movement (following their teacher-in-role wearing different attire), copying sequences of sounds (joining in the refrain), listening and attending to rhymes, stories and simple recounts linked to sensory cues (following the retelling of the 'Three Little Pigs' tale), sustaining attention in different activities (the variety of chores in between the regular refrain in the PDS) and responding to instructions (in order to carry out their chosen task effectively). (Based on QCA 2001b.)

Additionally, the QCA (2001b) emphasises the importance of developing the ability of all children with learning difficulties to respond to the communication of others and to develop *joint attention* through group discussion and interaction opportunities. Drama can be particularly beneficial for children with autism in this respect, as they particularly struggle with this perception of 'joint attention' on a shared object or experience as intrinsically holding 'something in it for them'. The Mrs Pig PDS illustrates how they may be required to:

- *take turns in a range of situations and for a variety of purposes,* for example, cooperating with others in a shared task (to complete Mrs Pig's chores), actively contributing to interactions (responding to direct approaches from their teacher-in-role, impelling them to action through her urgency), and maintaining interaction through more than one turn (her persistence to sustain repeated communicative exchanges, focused on a clear task in hand).
- *initiate communication,* for example, through smiling, making eye contact, reaching out, touching, or drawing attention to an object or event of interest (teacher-in-role harnessing the focused opportunity to invest meaning into their spontaneous reactions). (Based on QCA 2001b.)

Social interaction (including working with others)

Children with autism are fundamentally challenged in their ability to appreciate the experience of others, to consider different perspectives and to benefit from what others think, say and do (Baron-Cohen 1993). Drama offers explicit opportunities for children with autism to learn how to 'mind read', by focusing on how to interpret responses of others, whether expressed verbally or non-verbally. They can thus also discover a sense of *intentionality*: how to make choices and decisions to influence other people; also how to make sense of the intentions of others from what they say – or do not say.

For example, in the above drama, the participants could focus explicitly on the body language of the official breaking the news about plans to develop Monet's garden. In particular, they may need to examine the significance of 'two-faced' body language – the ambiguous big smile. The teacher (in role alongside the 'gardeners', listening to an assistant in role as the official) could even shout freeze: pausing the drama momentarily, to 'unpack' (out of role) the official's expression, and discuss implications.

An important life-skill for children with autism is to learn to cooperate and work effectively with others, both in formal and informal settings. Drama offers opportunities for children with autism to develop several aspects to this key skill:

- *developing social skills,* for example, awareness and/or tolerance of others (taking part in a group experience), empathy and awareness of the feelings and perspectives of others (responding constructively to the needs of Mrs Pig), turn-taking (ritualised activity), sharing (using communal classroom equipment), getting a balance between listening and responding (judging when to join in with the familiar ditty and being quiet in between), negotiating and supporting (choosing an activity that has not yet been carried out).
- *gaining, maintaining or directing the attention of others,* for example, vocalising or signing to ask to join in a group activity (indicating they wish to have a turn next at the appropriate moment).

- *adopting and accepting different roles appropriate to the setting* (appropriate social behaviour to Mrs Pig).
- *recognising the rules and conventions of different groups in formal and informal settings according to the size of the group* (behaving politely as a guest in Mrs Pig's house – not shouting out, sitting patiently, remembering appropriate greeting in response to her 'good morning' and 'goodbye').
- *recognising a common purpose*, for example, working together to create a scene in drama. (Based on QCA 2001a.)

Social interaction skills can be promoted directly through the way the drama is organised. It is possible to encourage children with autism to collaborate by using structures that intrinsically demand cooperation and negotiation; for example, a movement exercise (Sherborne 1990), a drama game (including Prescribed Drama Structures), a physical task or a ritual. Their attention may be so riveted on the task that they are able to tolerate the physical proximity of others. To a greater or lesser degree, all children with autism will struggle to sustain interaction within the make-believe, but it may be possible to enable them to stay 'with' the action, and to negotiate and cooperate through strategic use of sensitive supporting staff.

The contribution of *supporting staff* in the drama will be crucial in helping children with autism acquire personal powers, and to exercise them in ways which are socially acceptable (Harris 1994). The essential 'game of theatre' (Bolton 1992) requires everyone to 'suspend their disbelief', and create an appropriate atmosphere in order to provide a framework within which the children's actions can be seen as having meaning. It is crucial therefore, that supporting staff are briefed, and that they are willing to make the drama work – the developing fiction can be very fragile, and is dependent on the staff to model appropriate 'play' responses.

Supporting adults also need to respond to the actions and utterances of the children as if they are expressions of intention, consistent with the unfolding fiction. This can require some quick thinking in order to make the contribution of a child with autism relevant, often by getting at the 'nub' of their intention, even if at first a comment may seem tangential. Often there may be an inherent logic to the comments of children with autism, and many may speak in an idiosyncratic 'code'. Staff may play a crucial part therefore, in enabling all participants to see the potential 'shared meaning' embedded in a range of contributions, and to build on this in a way that is perceived as relevant by everyone. It may be possible to raise the self-esteem of children with autism by acting on their initiative within the lesson, and so elevate a particular child's status within the group.

Supporting staff may also have another important function: helping children with autism to conceptualise alternative outcomes, and supporting them in compromising or negotiating over choices. This can be particularly problematic, owing to their relative inflexibility and rigidity of thought. Through drama they may be enabled to learn that other people have personal powers too, and learn also how to become aware of the likely desires and interests of other people in a range of social contexts.

Children with autism may need to realise and accept that their own personal powers are necessarily limited according to a particular situation, and learn how to maximise them according to context (talking politely to a teacher-in-role rather than trying to obtain something by shouting or screaming). Drama offers unique learning opportunities in this regard for expressing and communicating meaning effectively. The following chapter will explore the potential of the art form of drama for children with autism for understanding how social meanings may be constructed. This will then enable them to use the narrative form as a powerful means to express and communicate a statement.

CHAPTER 6

Learning *in* Drama: play with meaning

This chapter shows how drama may be used with children with autism to enable them to understand how social meanings are constructed. This may be achieved by consciously 'deconstructing' the drama form – for example, aspects of language, movement and gesture, use of space. A range of options is also presented – drama strategies and conventions – at the teacher's disposal for organising drama work, with particular reference to their usefulness with children with autism at different stages of development in their play potential.

Crucially, drama needs to be pitched at a level that is appropriate to the development of the participants, if children are to access the shared meanings inherent in the content. The requirement here is for the teacher to select aspects of the theatre form and drama conventions that will enable the children to engage with the content; it is this that will give depth, quality and significance to the experience. It is the teacher's responsibility therefore, to ensure *maximum engagement* by the participants with the drama activity.

Children with autism and the art form of drama

During the drama itself, the focus of attention will necessarily be on the creation of the fictitious context, and at times on the actual drama form used to give shape to the experience; learning as such will occur at a level of subsidiary awareness. However, this cannot be left *implicit*, and will need to be raised to the forefront of the consciousness of children with autism – made *explicit* – by discussing the drama afterwards. Connections will need to be made between the make-believe situation and real life. This detachment from the dramatic activity is a double-featured process:

- detaching oneself from the content in order to examine it and learn from it;

- detaching oneself from the theatre form in order to examine how something was achieved (Bolton 1992: 117).

For children with autism, unravelling aspects of the theatre form to see how they are being manipulated will provide unique insights and learning opportunities. By exploring how meanings are created in the drama situation, and by reflecting objectively and explicitly on these out of role, children with autism may be enabled to make connections from the make-believe to real life. Learning about meanings may occur both in and out of role, on both real and symbolic levels. Social meanings are constructed through manipulations of:

- verbal and non-verbal language;
- use of space and time;
- the creation of tension in different ways.

Language

Drama is a group experience, and depends upon the creative interaction between the participants, both on the real dimension (planning, discussing, organising, reviewing), and on the symbolic level (temporarily interacting within the make-believe). Verbal language may be used within the group outside the drama, and also symbolically to represent a situation or what a particular character says within the drama. Non-verbal communication may also be appropriate, using movement, symbols and visual imagery.

Drama offers children with autism a range of possible naturalistic contexts in which to practise their *communication skills*: particular vocabulary, maybe using a language construction correctly in order to obtain something, and selecting the appropriate form of message and language for a particular audience, situation or purpose. Different contexts in the drama may present new language challenges, with the teacher possibly introducing these in process, to be explored afterwards in more structured learning contexts.

In drama, children with autism can be directly confronted with the relationship between their communication skills and the effect on others, with the use of role protecting the children from untoward consequences. For example, drama may provide a variety of social situations in which to master the productive use of direct and indirect speech acts, for instance finding a tactful excuse to leave ('I promised to be home for tea'), rather than declaring 'I'm bored with your company and I want to go' (Harris 1994). The drama emotionally protects the children should a 'social *faux pas*' be made: it would be the *role* – the person the child was pretending to be, however notional, rather than the child directly – who was responsible for causing offence.

Similarly, *subtleties of interaction* – communication competence skills – can be explored safely in the drama, so that children with autism may learn to develop what is relevant in conversation and inhibit inappropriate contributions. These will include making appropriate comments, turn taking, organising ideas logically and concisely and socially appropriate body language. For example, a teacher-in-role may be legitimately irritated by a child mumbling, and so impel the child (in role) to find a more appropriate manner!

Time and space

Drama explores notions of 'elastic time': the drama may unfold at life pace, or be stopped, accelerated and replayed. Potentially this may be very confusing for children with autism; however, if they can learn to *relate to shifting concepts of time* in drama, this may actually help them grasp how events in the real world relate to one another, and help them begin to understand and predict the consequences of human actions and behaviour. Moving between different time dimensions will need to be made very clear for children with autism; for example, using a demarcated part of the drama space to represent an incident in the past (possibly enhanced by lighting). They will also need to be talked through what is happening quite explicitly: 'Let's pretend we've been on our bus journey, and we've now arrived at the beach – it's a lovely sunny afternoon (turn up the lights in that part of the drama space).'

Chapter 7 explores narrative in depth and illustrates how developing drama as if it was a video recording can be enormously helpful: in this way, children with autism may be enabled to grasp how time can be manipulated in drama. This may actually prompt them to enjoy the predictability of being able to *control time* in drama, in the same way as they often enjoy playing video tapes for this reason. For example, 'rewinding' or doing an 'action replay' of a scene that has just taken place, allows moments to be revisited and subjected to scrutiny. If this is too confusing, then perhaps recording the lesson on video may enable children with autism to understand the convention of time in drama, if the previous lesson is then developed in a future one, and so becomes a 'rolling drama'. This may well be within the grasp of children with autism, through their exposure to the soap opera genre on TV!

Similarly, *use of space* may be analysed in order for children with autism to understand how meanings are created, both symbolically in the drama and also in real life. For example, there is the psychological distance in certain social relationships, signalled by everyone standing, saluting and bowing in the presence of an authority figure. Children with autism may come to have expectations from a regular 'acting space' or set, as a place where meanings will be created. In this way, they may discover the potential of using a space for enhancing shared meaning and building belief.

Children with autism may need to be helped into the symbolism, especially at first, and to become actively involved in adapting the environment and creating the set for the drama – also returning the room to its original state after the drama. Indeed, elaborate sets may be perceived as 'real' as opposed to realistic by children with autism. Starting with a 'blank' set can be more constructive, so that participants may contribute ideas and initiatives to block out areas. For example, 'Where shall we put this blue cloth, which will be the river?' . . . 'How close to one another should these two characters stand if they don't like each other?'

Dramatic tension

The key theatre element to creating a quality experience in drama is *dramatic tension*, which is something that both teacher and children have to learn to sense, control and manipulate. It is also the key to enabling children with autism to understand their own feelings and those of others, and to learn how to control and manipulate their reactions. Dramatic tension is the 'motor' that drives the drama, that gives narrative its momentum. It is in these moments of disequilibrium that participants are put on their mettle, challenged and prompted to respond to events outside their existing frame of reference. It is the tension and pressure experienced in these key moments, that provides a sense of urgency that impels them into action to resolve the situation, by making choices or decisions. Reflecting afterwards can put children with autism directly in touch with their own reactions and those of others, and enable them to consider consequences: for example, 'What was it in the drama that made us feel scared?' . . . . 'What happened when we screamed at [Shirley] when she was pretending to be the Bear?'

In order for the tension to be experienced, signals from the teacher will need to be very clear, blatant and uncomplicated; children with autism will struggle with subtleties of communication, such as a raising of the eyebrows. Likewise the teacher's own language will need to be explicit and avoid ambiguity. Tension may be created through (for example):

- *use of contrast* (moments of darkness followed by light, stillness then movement, quiet then noise, fast activity followed by slow, free use of space then confined);
- *deliberate use of symbols* (picture of a missing person, salvaged flag from a shipwreck, a letter);
- *situation* (a sudden surprise or unexpected turn of events, a limitation or constraint imposed);
- *manipulating time* (a delaying tactic, or a sudden sense of urgency to resolve a crisis).

In order to sustain and generate tension and a sense of urgency, drama has to have an appropriate *rhythm and pace*, and will need to be finely tuned. Children with autism may find it alarming to have sudden 'surprises' injected into the drama, although a sudden acceleration in pace may prompt them into a response. An ebb and flow of energy levels using a variety of drama conventions, will help focus attention and enable those children with short concentration spans to come and go. Opportunities for reflection within the drama as well as out of role, will be crucial in enabling children with autism to stay engaged with the meaning, and to see the relevance to real life situations.

Belief in the dramatic tension will be enhanced by staff creating an *appropriate atmosphere*, not only by generating and modelling appropriate responses, but also by the use of physical devices (lighting, special effects, costume, etc.). It will be important however, that the physical limitations and constraints of the particular setting are observed and respected, as this will fundamentally affect the creation of an appropriate atmosphere; this fragility can be shattered by an unforeseen interruption to the running of the session. For example, teachers will need to consider timetabling pressures on the drama space, timings for school transport, noise thresholds, commitments of the pupils (for example, various therapies or individual one-to-one sessions). Certain drama conventions (ways of organising the drama) may also hold their own inherent tension.

Children with autism – engaging with the content

Engaging with the drama on a feeling level will be critical for children with autism to sense and relate to something 'other' than their usual frame of reference. Children at different stages of development in their understanding of symbolism and narrative will have varying abilities to access meanings in drama in different ways. Symbolic understanding actually need not be a prerequisite for meaningful participation in drama (Bolton 1986). Peter (1994, 1995) and Grove and Park (2001) demonstrate how children at earlier stages of learning may have their play appropriately differentiated within (inclusive) imaginary drama contexts. This premise is also fundamental to play-drama intervention: the 'learn how to do it while doing it' approach.

Drama strategies

Certain teaching strategies, particuarly questioning, discussion and reflection, are crucial in facilitating meaningful engagement of children with autism within the drama.

Questioning

In drama work, teachers are often exhorted to use *open questions* to empower children, for example: 'How can we make our plan better?' However, children with autism may find these too vague and threatening and struggle with the mental agility required. Paradoxically they may be empowered through the offer of tighter boundaries within which to contribute a creative response. Teachers really need to develop a *hierarchy of questioning skills*, perhaps starting with an open question, and then narrowing the focus as required. Despite their bad press, *closed questions* (demanding a yes/no response) may have specific application and usefulness for children with autism, and may not always be as limiting as they appear! Closed questions can be used strategically, and can even offer a child the opportunity to change the direction of a drama. For example:

- *as a quick cross-check of facts* – for example, 'Was the official nice? Yes or no?'
- *to create a sense of urgency* – for example, 'You will help me do my jobs, won't you?'
- *to gain attention* – for example, 'Do you like these pictures?'
- *to remind about the task in hand* – for example, 'Is this a good way to go past a dinosaur?'
- *to gain consensus* – for example, 'Do you think we should make a plan then?'
- *to empower certain pupils to make a creative decision* – for example, 'Shall we all write a letter then? Yes or no? OK . . . '

Discussion

This will be crucial to ensure that children with autism have grasped the significance of an unfolding drama, especially as their response may be somewhat idiosyncratic. Discussion will enable ideas to be consolidated and clarified as necessary, although care should be taken to prevent this becoming tedious and overworked, which will risk participants losing concentration or 'switching off'. Discussion can take place *within* the drama in role, for example, contriving a *meeting* (very useful for slowing it down, preventing children from rushing headlong, and for helping them think through the implications of their suggestions). Discussion should also take place out of role, *before* the drama (exploring the topic for the drama and in constructing the make-believe context), and *after* the drama, to consolidate learning areas explored.

Reflection

This is important both within the drama and afterwards, for consolidating learning. Use of objects of reference, props and video footage may help prompt memory and recall of a drama experience. Sometimes, learning may not be apparent immediately, but may emerge some time afterwards, in a spontaneous free-play opportunity. In process, the teacher will need to find ways to bring a significant moment to the attention of the participants, usually through a thoughtful, contemplative task that will slow down the action. Children with autism will need the focus explained; it is unrealistic to rely on them engaging intuitively with an implicit meaning. Examples of reflection opportunities may include:

- *Pausing the action momentarily* – for example, 'while you are doing your job, think about some of the dangers that face people like the Flintstones'.
- *Writing in role* – for example, composing a letter of complaint about proposed plans for Monet's garden, explaining their reasons for their protest.
- *A ritual* – for example, each person focusing on the mysterious official, shaking hands in turn.
- *Drawing a picture* – for example, a design for a landscaped car park, showing necessary changes to Monet's garden to make room for the visitors' cars.
- *Writing afterwards* – for example, an account of what happened in the Flintstones drama, and how they might deal with a dangerous looking animal in real life.
- *Playing out events afterwards* – offering opportunities to revisit events from the drama spontaneously, perhaps with key props made available to support the children with autism in making meanings.

Drama conventions

A choice of drama conventions is at the teacher's disposal for organising the make-believe in order to give it shape. Some drama conventions are simply more challenging than others, although all may be usefully revisited at more advanced levels, differentiated and enjoyed by inclusive groups. These are described briefly below, along with other dimensions that characterise the responses in drama of children with autism at different stages of their play development. It is possible to track how these may develop into a profile for progression in drama (see Figure 6.1). However, 'teacher-in-role' is by far the most valuable drama convention for working with children with autism and merits special consideration.

Teaching in role
The teacher-in-role can readily capture the *interest and joint attention* of children with autism, especially when this is enhanced through effective performance and attractive, strategic use of props. In order to convey signals through role clearly, acting skills are required to make the signals blatant. It can be a fine balance, between avoiding ambiguity and going over the top and hamming up the role! The important thing is to be clear about the meaning that is to be conveyed, and to think of using the role simply as a mantle or teaching tool to enter the make-believe. Using a simple prop or item of costume (hat, apron, clipboard) can help signal to the children when you are talking in role; this is particularly important for

children with autism, to enable them to learn from drama's 'double edge' – doing drama with a clear awareness that it is make-believe. Make sure that props or items are not cumbersome, and can be quickly and easily removed; if the whole thing degenerates into pantomime, this will result in focus being lost.

Secondly, teaching in role on the inside of the drama enables material to be explored in the 'here and now', with a directness and immediacy for manipulating *emotional engagement* and accessing meaning. The key is for the teacher to find an appropriate role to operate inside the drama that will enable the participants to contribute ideas and gain insights. There is no need to 'feel stuck' in a role: if it feels obsolete, it can be discarded or transferred to another person (supporting member of staff or a child), easily signified if a simple prop is used. Several options are possible:

- *A low status role* – someone in need of the group's help or expertise; for example, Mrs Pig, desperate for assistance with her housework.
- *A high status role* – an authority figure who impels respect, control or appropriate behaviour; for example, the official announcing development plans for Monet's garden.
- *An agent* – someone carrying out orders or instructions, who may become a potential ally for the group; for example, teacher-in-role as head gardener in Monet's garden.
- *A stranger* – someone to whom the group are obliged to explain themselves; for example, a news reporter who comes to interview the gardeners about their reactions to proposed developments for Monet's garden.
- *Indeterminate role* – which may become clear-cut later on; for example the anonymous teacher-in-role questioning the group as they set about their tasks in the Flintstones drama, who later balks their quick-fix plans by his or her cowardice.
- A *negative role* – teacher-in-role is deliberately inept at a particular task: the children might not be able to tell you what to do, but they may well be able to tell or show the teacher in role what *not* to do; for example, not to stamp past a sleeping dinosaur!

Thirdly, the teacher-in-role is able to *structure the narrative* and give form to the emerging make-believe from within, without breaking the fragile fiction that is being created. Concentration and group dynamic may easily be lost with children with autism otherwise. Working in role also helps circumvent complex language constructions: instead of 'What would you do if . . . .', this can be immediately played out 'for real'. Teacher-in-role has many uses:

- *Moving pupils quickly into the drama* – Mrs Pig immediately set the context.
- *Presenting an opposing viewpoint* – the inept character in the Flintstones drama.

	SENSORI-MOTOR and RELATIONAL PLAY	FUNCTIONAL and Emergent SYMBOLIC PLAY	SYMBOLIC and SOCIODRAMATIC PLAY	Spontaneous imaginary and THEMED FANTASY PLAY
PERCEPTUAL INTEREST	Exploration of objects, props Teacher in (low status or negative) role Children in notional roles, mantle of the expert Joint attention on shared focus – tolerating being part of the group, involvement in collaborative tasks	Familiar or shared story, TV programme or play routine Teacher in (high status) role Children in collective roles – use of objects/props in pretence Actively participating in and out of role	Range of representational stimuli (pictures, music, objects) Teacher in (agent or indeterminate) role Children in individual roles (stock responses) – use of objects symbolically Communicating in and out of role – answering questions in role	Narrative/text/play sequence as stimuli Teacher in role selectively or ambiguously Individual character roles with versatility – use of imaginary objects Negotiating in and out of role, considering others – posing questions in role
AFFECTIVE ENGAGEMENT	Expression of feeling (to changes in atmosphere or to consequences of action) that influences the context Acknowledgement of cause-effect situations with immediate consequences – recollecting the drama afterwards Expansion of shared interest perceiving personal relevance	Expression of intention/desire - awareness of own feeling state Understanding of motive and cause-effect consequences Taking a perspective – expressing an opinion	Recognition of the connection between mental states and consequent behaviour Having insight into themes and issues – making connections to real life Interacting within the make-believe with respect for others	Appreciating mental states of others – having a sense of 'audience' Encapsulating a meaning by using the drama form Spontaneous, self-generated play responses
PLAY/ TEACHING STRUCTURE	Imitation of a routine Structured choice making towards a clear goal Clear-cut, brief activities:	More flexible attitude to narrative – carrying out a short, familiar sequence Practical problem-solving 'Living through' simple narratives:	Opportunity to consider implication of mental states and consequent behaviour More complex problem-solving using prediction/persuasion Interacting in more complex, flexible narratives:	Understanding the complexity and implications of mixed feelings for themselves and others Coping with a dilemma or where no clear solution exists Appreciation of others' mental states in theatre presentation:
DRAMA CONVENTIONS	Prescribed drama structure, drama games Ritual, rehearsal Movement Cross-curricular tasks, arts activities	Open-ended PDS Structured play Freeze-frame, 'fast-forwarding' Teacher-led improvisation – use of narrative links and teacher talkover	Pair/group improvisation Creating rehearsed improvised sequence 'Rewinding', 'action-replay' Thought-tracking	Hot-seating, forum theatre Creating play scripts Frozen tableaux Conscience alley, doubling

Play activity →
Purposeful engagement →

Figure 6.1 Progression in drama

- *Providing a focus for attention* – the mysterious official in Monet's garden.
- *Providing an appropriate model of behaviour* – the head gardener in Monet's garden.
- *Presenting challenges* – the head gardener spurring the group to come up with a strategy in the light of the development plans for Monet's garden.
- *Multiplying options within the drama* by gaining an extra person or lifestyle – development plans for Monet's garden being issued directly face-to-face rather than indirectly through the written word or reported speech.

Sensori-motor/relational play

Children with autism at these early stages of their play development benefit from teaching structures that involve *expansion* and *modelled routines*; these can be built in to a drama experience, even if other meanings within the make-believe are at a more advanced level of symbolic understanding. This entails joining the children in whatever captures their interests, and extending this by explicitly demonstrating an action for the child to imitate, in order to build up a simple routine. This is significant for developing their self-awareness as well as awareness of others. Moments can be framed through making eye contact, and establishing mutual gaze, before repeating a particular activity within the drama.

It is important that children are given a *notional role* within the drama, so that they are necessarily caught up in the action. *Teacher-in-role* can help set the frame for this, so that children play themselves caught up in the experience (for example, greeting them in role as Mrs Pig, the children playing an undefined role, but nevertheless firmly within the fiction). It is better at first, for children simply to focus on their feeling responses, rather than on the implications of playing a character part. Sympathetic, appealing low status roles in need of help are less likely to feel threatening to the children. Using negative role may also be effective: children at these early stages may well be intrigued by the incongruity of their teacher dressed up and seemingly doing the 'wrong thing'.

A drama context can offer opportunities to develop *joint attention* on attractive or intriguing objects, and share in a group experience; their attention may be so riveted on a particular prop or character (especially a teacher-in-role), that the children may find themselves tolerating this social dimension inadvertently! Drama lends itself to use of appealing, multi-sensory props and frippery to create the make-believe, which may offer children possibilities to develop *emotional responses* and express their feelings within an exciting and stimulating context. They may also respond to changes in atmosphere, created by physical adaptation to the drama space (lighting, for example), and also the other-world 'buzz' of the drama experience. Strongly contrastive experiences may help the formation of sensory images and associations in memory (Grove and Park 2001).

Drama contexts can also help children with autism at these early stages of play development, to develop a sense of themselves as active agents, capable of exerting influence on their environment, through making clearly defined choices. This goal-directed, *cause–effect* behaviour can be encouraged by actions with particular props, or to another character within the drama. Spontaneous actions should be reinforced directly by staff in role so that the child immediately experiences the consequences, and actions should be extended through supporting staff demonstrating other possibilities. In order to consolidate the experience and their awareness of their own involvement and participation, children at these early stages should be encouraged to *recall* the drama in order to strengthen their autobiographical memory. Use of video, photographs and visual cues (drama props) may be useful prompts to enable the child to lock in to the experience.

Drama structures appropriate for this level need to be clear-cut, tightly structured, relatively short activities. While these may seem limiting, paradoxically, they can be very enabling for children to learn to make a creative choice within clear, secure boundaries. These activities can often work at many levels of ability (provided they are differentiated to offer an appropriate level of challenge to the participants), so are useful in groups with diverse learning needs. They also help focus attention, and so can be effective with those children with autism who are at more advanced stages of play development but who may have short concentration spans.

Examples include:

- *Warm-up drama games* – the 'hot potato' game prior to the Monet's garden lesson.
- *Prescribed Drama Structures* – Mrs Pig drama; also the example in the Monet's garden lesson.
- *Ritual* – consolidating the group experience by everyone performing a specific action: everyone in turn formally greets the official in the Monet's garden drama with a shake of the hand and 'bonjour'.
- *Movement experiences* – creating a human escape tunnel, everyone in a line on hands and knees, in the Flintstone drama.
- *Cross-curricular tasks* – matching photographs with corresponding real items in the Mrs Pig PDS; writing a letter in role in the Monet's garden drama.
- *Rehearsal* – practising a skill to be used later in the drama: practising tip-toe before each person in turn has to move past the sleeping dinosaur.
- *Cross-arts activities* – where art, music, writing or dance are integral to the drama, as in creating designs for a landscaped car park for Monet's garden at Giverny.

Functional/emergent symbolic play
For children with autism at these stages of their play development, teaching structures need to encourage them to build up routines into short sequences, and

develop simple *narrative* frameworks. Familiar stories, TV programmes, favourite videos or established play routines can be useful starting points for drama work. Changes may be sensitively introduced to the anticipated structure, to encourage the children to develop a more *flexible* approach to narrative; for example, opening up a PDS. Children at these stages will require explicit teaching of the representational use of objects and pretend actions, in order to develop their emergent symbolic understanding; opportunities can be afforded within the drama context itself, through appropriate choice of conventions and strategies.

At these levels of their play development, children may consciously take on collective roles (workers, villagers). It may be particularly empowering to adopt the *mantle of the expert*: to be in a position to offer help or expertise to a *teacher-in-role*. In addition to the use of low status characters and negative role, it may be possible to challenge the children through use of teacher-in-role as a high status authority figure, who commands respect and a response from them.

Children at these stages of their play development can follow an unfolding storyline, and should be supported in beginning to take a perspective. While they may make stock responses to developments within the drama, they will need to be made explicitly aware of their emotional state and resulting actions; also to recognise these in others. They should be encouraged to express intentions and desires, and to make straightforward decisions and solve simple problems (for example, requiring a baldly practical solution) within more open-ended drama contexts.

Drama structures at these levels of development in play should aim to sustain a clear sense of unfolding narrative, and seek to enable children with autism to engage with meanings in the drama on a feeling level. Developing a clear sense of detachment from the make-believe (for example, pausing the drama momentarily) may support a growing awareness of the pretend make-believe context in the drama.

Examples include those above, plus:

- *Open-ended PDS* – unexpectedly changing the anticipated outcome, to create an open-ended situation for the children to resolve.
- *Structured play* – the teacher helps to organise who is doing what and where, and helps the participants focus and stay on task through sensitive, probing questioning about their role and the activities in which they are engaged. For example, in the Flintstone drama, one boy said he was making an arrow. The teacher asked him 'Where does arrow-making take place? Show me the space where that happens . . . Is it over here? . . . Or here? Who helps you make arrows?'
- *Miming* to the teacher's narration using real objects.
- *Teacher talk-over* – teacher narrates while the children improvise, so providing

possible 'hooks' to keep them focused (for example, 'It was an ordinary day for the Flintstones . . . some of their friends were busy making arrows, others were preparing a meal . . .).

- *Improvisation* – developing their symbolic play in process, in a teacher-led, whole group drama, with strategic use of supporting staff. Tasks at this level need to be very clear cut, and well within children's everyday experience. Using props (real objects) as a focus will support them in accessing the significance (as for the household tasks in the Mrs Pig PDS); supporting staff in role may present alternative approaches to a particular task.
- *Freeze frame* – pausing the drama momentarily at a high point of tension, to draw attention to its significance.
- *Narrative links* – succinct, unwordy teacher input, to connect scenes and move the drama on (for example, 'and so it was that . . . .').
- *Stopping the drama* – useful for a quick cross-check to make sure everyone is 'with it' before resuming role (for example, teacher could ask 'Who was I pretending to be when I had this hat on just now?'); also for discussing possible lines of development.

Symbolic/sociodramatic play

At this level of their play development, children with autism will have a rudimentary ability to engage in symbolic play, with a clear grasp of narrative. They will require their play to become more flexible and dynamic in *interactive* situations, developed from the play of other people, and so may gain considerably from the opportunities presented to create shared meanings within drama. At this stage, the children should be encouraged to use object substitution – using real objects to stand for something else; also to mime pretend actions with greater respect for the properties of imaginary objects. Their more flexible view of narrative may enable them to approach the unfolding drama in different directions, moving forwards or backwards in time – fast forwarding, rewinding or doing an 'action replay' to repeat a scene.

At this stage of their play development, the interest and attention of children with autism may be captured initially through a range of possible stimuli. These may have representational significance: for example, intriguing objects, pictures, extracts of music. They may begin to take on individual character roles, albeit in a rather perfunctory manner, and be able to hold belief sufficiently to relate to a teacher-in-role as an agent or indeterminate role, such as a stranger. At this stage too, the children may be encouraged to interact with one another more, both in and out of role. They may be challenged to answer questions in role, and to reflect on developments both within the drama and afterwards, showing insight into themes and issues being explored. The children should also be encouraged explicitly to make connections from the situation in the drama to analogous situations in the real world.

Specifically too, children with autism at this stage in their play development need to consolidate their awareness of the connection between desires, beliefs and emotional states and ensuing actions and behaviour. They will require explicit opportunities within the drama, to develop recognition of others' feelings and intentions as well as their own. They should also be encouraged to express their thoughts, feelings, ideas and opinions, and to begin to think through the implications of their suggestions. They may be challenged with more complex problem solving, involving prediction and persuasion, and should be encouraged to listen to the views and opinions of others, and to reach group decisions.

Drama structures at this stage need to capitalise on the children's growing ability to relate to others and to cope with the unexpected. Judicious grouping of children with autism within the drama may enable them to communicate and negotiate with others. It may be prudent to facilitate this initially with sensitivity to group dynamics: preferred personalities, and tolerance of particular individuals and working spaces, in order to maximise possibilities for interaction.

Examples include all the above, plus:

- *Improvisation – pairs/group work –* tasks that intrinsically require more than one person; for example, one person washing up, the other drying.
- *Creating a short rehearsed improvisation –* a short script (spoken or written) devised to express a significant meaning (not necessarily for an audience).
- *Thought-tracking –* speaking thoughts aloud in role, possibly using paper 'think bubbles' or 'speech bubbles'.

Spontaneous/themed fantasy play

At this stage it is possible that certain children with autism may have reached a more advanced level of symbolic understanding and play development. They may be able to engage in *role play* and *sustain belief* in a narrative, with increasing flexibility, imagination and spontaneity and in *interactive* scenarios. They will need contexts within the drama, which will prompt them to engage in this internally generated, *spontaneous* imaginative play, including responding to the comments of others. They will benefit from opportunities within the drama to maximise their growing ability to *communicate* with others, and may be expected to mime with respect for *imagined* properties of real or non-existent objects or characters, and symbolic use of space.

The interest of children at this more advanced stage of their symbolic understanding may be captivated by narrative itself as a stimulus: a picture story book or written text, or a piece of theatre. Children at this stage of their play development may be capable of taking on individual roles with growing flexibility and versatility, and to convey more subtle expression of emotion, through their use of posture, voice and movement. They may be challenged by taking on a variety of roles, with characters that change and develop. Similarly, they may engage with a teacher-in-role playing a more ambiguous character – someone who is two-faced, for example. They will need to be supported in understanding the complexity of these characters and in appreciating the implications of mixed feelings for their own behaviour and that of others.

The growing sensitivity in social situations of children at this stage may be further challenged, by creating opportunities in the drama where they are required to negotiate with their peers in and out of role (perhaps with staff supporting less overtly), and demonstrate consideration and receptiveness to the ideas of others. Their ability to cope more flexibly in situations may enable them to deal with dilemmas being presented in the drama: to offer original suggestions, and to consider different possible outcomes to resolve problems that are less clear-cut. They may also be able to suggest ways to organise the drama in order to explore an issue (use of space, time, pace, lighting, etc.).

Drama structures at this level may capitalise on the children's developing 'theory of mind', and their growing ability to appreciate the mental states of others. This will make possible the use of drama conventions that require a sense of audience: where meanings are encapsulated and shared explicitly with others within a short presentation, and with an awareness of their likely impact. This mind-leap of course is very challenging for children with autism, although it may be within the grasp of some. Watching presentations, however, can be very useful at all levels of play development, and these moments of 'theatre' can be deconstructed in order to access meaning.

Examples include all of the above, plus:

Reading a letter – character in role conveys a significant development.

Making a phone call – tension created by what is said, not said, or the character's reactions.

Creating a frozen image or tableau – significant moments captured at the height of their potential impact.

Hot-seating – questioning a character in role about their experiences, actions, behaviour.

Conscience alley – as with thought tracking, but the children stand in two lines facing one another; as a character walks down the aisle, the 'walls' voice aloud thoughts or advice to the person.

Doubling – placing hand on the shoulder of another character, and voicing how that character might be feeling.

Forum theatre – audience and performers negotiate the direction for the unfolding drama.

Group sculpt – creating a shape to express an aspect of the theme being explored.

Scripting plays – written or improvised, autonomously or in pairs or small groups, in order to devise a new context to present an idea, theme or issue.

Play with meaning

Drama thrives on a growing awareness of one's personal powers for manipulating emotions and concepts in relation to other people. This may occur on two levels: in the make-believe itself, using symbols and metaphors to convey meaning (ideas, thoughts and feelings), and also on a real level, through direct participation with and alongside others. Analysing how aspects of the theatre form are manipulated to give depth and quality to a fictitious life situation in drama will give insight into how social meanings are constructed in the real world. Children's growing understanding and use of the art form of drama through structured teaching may empower them to harness narrative (use of symbols and metaphors) to extend their social experience; the following chapter explores how this may be developed in children with autism.

CHAPTER 7

Learning *about* Drama: play with a purpose

Consistent with the approach advocated hitherto for play-drama intervention, this chapter illustrates how drama can offer a structured approach and an inside-out means for children to advance their understanding of narrative – perceived by some to be a major 'stumbling block' in the development of children with autism (Bruner and Feldman 1993). It offers a practical, inclusive approach to teaching children about the relationship between narrative and text, and ways to access meaning in stories.

Ultimately, it may be that certain children with autism can learn how to use narrative to craft a script (spoken and/or written) in order to express and communicate a shared meaning. Strategies are offered to support them in developing their playwriting skills, together with suggestions for using existing text as a stimulus for devising their own work.

Drama: making meanings

Previous chapters have identified the potential of drama to explore moments when someone is 'in a mess', having to cope with attitudes, issues, dilemmas, or resolve problems of human experience. The 'Flintstones' drama considered ways to cope effectively with a potentially dangerous animal, while the 'Three Little Pigs' drama explored implications of the life-style of a busy home-maker, by encouraging participants to empathise proactively with Mrs Pig, an otherwise forgotten character. Both these lessons were developed from a familiar 'script', and deviated from the storyline 'as known' to develop a more flexible narrative structure. This in itself constituted significant, fundamental learning for the child with autism: the notion that things can be different, and that the child can be instrumental in causing that to be so. Also, the idea that 'conflict' – feelings of unease – are part of what constitutes being in the world, and that compromises can be worked at and agreed, and resolutions found.

Drama can move children with autism closer to fiction and understanding of an existing text. Significant moments (shared meanings embedded within the text) can be explored, so helping them find forms to communicate their personal and collective responses that go beyond the literal (Baldwin 1998). *Character, setting* and *plot* are the organising concepts of text (as recognised in the National Literacy Strategy, DfEE 1998), but are also the structural components of drama. In drama, participants at all levels are confronted with a *character* (who is this drama about?): his or her appearance, personal qualities, actions, behaviour, feelings and relationships with others; also who they themselves are playing, and the staff's assumed roles and the nature of their fictitious relationships. Participants in drama have to take into account the *setting* (where is the drama taking place?) both in time and in space, and its influence on the characters. They will also experience what happens – the *plot* – the sequence of events, spurred along by its 'imperative tension' (Bolton 1992). The plot of most drama, at whatever level of sophistication, will have an opening phase to set the context, then a deepening phase that leads to a build-up of tension, culminating in a climax or conflict (which may occur suddenly or gradually), followed by a resolution by the characters concerned. This of course is the same structure that underpins the planning of any drama lesson, as indicated previously.

Drama explores 'stories' of human experience, albeit through analogous life-situations, so enabling children with autism to begin to understand from the inside something of the motives behind events, and how one situation can lead to another. Drama entails the creation – or re-creation – of a script: a sequence of events, each with its own inherent tensions that spur along the storyline. This script can be captured – written down, recorded on audio or videotape, or represented pictorially as a story board of drawings or photographs. A supporting member of staff could usefully video a drama lesson, which can then be re-played to the children as a complete narrative, and be used as a vehicle for discussing issues and inherent meanings. Working individually, in small groups or as a whole class, children with autism can also create a storyboard or written script for significant moments, either directly from memory, or using the video, objects of reference (key props) and discussion to prompt recall. These scripts may then themselves be used to re-create those significant moments. In this way, children with autism may be brought to a closer understanding that narrative structure originates in shared meanings created in action, and can be embedded in a visual or written *text*.

Understanding narrative

In order to reveal meanings embedded in narrative, it is necessary to go beyond a familiar storyline. Otherwise, there is a risk of the anticipation of what will be happening next in the sequence of events, and a superficial preoccupation with characterisation. A more flexible narrative is required: a series of incidents or events linked sequentially that can actually be recounted in different ways (see Figure 7.1). This approach to developing drama from story is explored in Peter (1996b). The narrative may be recounted by:

- working *forwards* in time: 'Once upon a time there was young girl called Cinderella, who lived with her mother and father . . . .'
- working *backwards* in time: 'there was once a beautiful queen called Cinderella, who came to marry the prince as he then was, because her foot fitted a glass slipper . . . '
- starting somewhere in the middle: 'there was once a magnificent ball held at the king's palace; all the people in the land were invited, but one person almost missed her chance . . .'

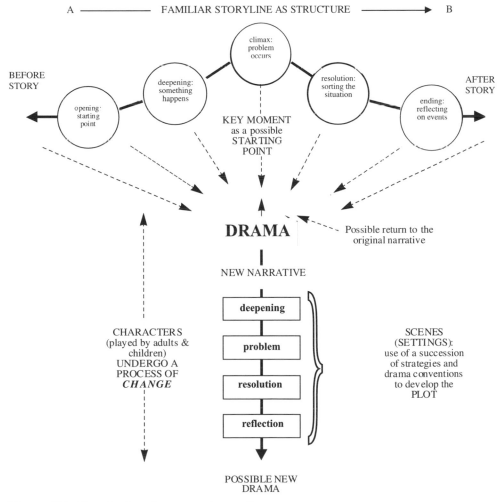

Figure 7.1 Developing drama and narrative

To access meanings in a story, any one of the key events in the narrative (when characters are usually under tension) may provide a starting point for developing drama work. These can be 'dipped into', before continuing forwards or backwards in time to explore a related incident. In the video age, children with autism – and indeed even those with severe learning difficulties – very often have a grasp of going with the convention in drama of 'elastic time': the idea that a narrative does not have to unfold at life pace, but can be 'fast-forwarded' or 'rewound'.

Potential learning areas will be raised by the particular story according to the meanings embedded in it; the teacher will need to balance these with the learning needs of the particular group. The question still remains however as to what should dictate the actual choice of the most viable moment in the story as a starting point for intervention through drama work. The following pointers may be helpful, here all linked to a popular children's picture story book (based on an original model by Sheppard, 1991 and 1994, and developed by Peter, 1996b).

Example: Where's My Teddy? (by Jez Alborough)

Where's My Teddy follows a little boy, Eddy, who wanders alone into the woods to look for his lost teddy bear. First of all he is puzzled to come across an enormous teddy . . . and then he encounters a giant bear also looking for his lost teddy, and clutching Eddy's tiny teddy . . . Both Eddy and the giant bear are mutually terrified of one another, and in the furore regain their respective bears, and rush home safely to bed!

Although it is actually a picture storybook aimed at young children, the issues and themes it raises are universal meanings that have relevance for all ages and abilities. Provided the book is presented appropriately, in a way that acknowledges participants' real ages, it actually offers learning potential through drama across the educational spectrum. For example, 'I'd like to read to you my little boy's favourite story. See if you can work out why he likes it so much.'

A particular character may offer a perspective on an issue or situation – forgotten characters (or those who might plausibly have been on the scene at the time) may present fertile material for drama; different characters would offer very different versions of the same story. Finding out where the character actually features most in key moments in the storyline may dictate which point in the narrative will provide a starting point for the drama. In *Where's My Teddy?*, Eddy's story would be different from the Bear's . . . What would be the version as told by Eddy's parent (or the Bear's parent)?

There may be a moral embedded in the story – many traditional folk tales contain some cultural imperative that is passed on from generation to generation; for example, Red Riding Hood, Goldilocks and Snow White all deal with 'stranger danger' themes. In fact, *Where's My Teddy?* also contains a very similar moral (shared meaning), regarding the dangers of wandering off alone into the woods. The teacher then will look to find a way to place the participants in the position of reflecting on the shared cultural meaning from within the drama. The teacher's own choice of role will be crucial – for example, playing a weak character (Eddy himself?) in need of advice from better informed, wiser 'others' (the group in a role reversal as friends of Eddy's mum?). Establishing where in the narrative this device may be used, will influence the point of intervention and starting point for drama.

Certain events may contain inherent tensions that beg more than passing consideration – certain moments in a story may be in danger of being 'glossed over', if the narrative is only considered from the perspective of a main protagonist; sometimes the illustrations can be carrying an important sub-text. In the case of *Where's My Teddy?*, both the illustrations and the written text are actually designed to challenge the negative stereotype that 'big' is necessarily 'bad' or 'hard': the giant bear too is vulnerable – he has feelings of being upset because he has lost something precious (his teddy), he is also scared (of small creatures such as Eddy!), and similarly needs to feel snuggly and secure in bed. Certain moments in the story therefore could actually offer a direct point of entry for exploring alternative perspectives in drama work.

The teacher may 'brainstorm' alternative ways of considering the story by asking a rhetorical question: 'what if. . . .?' This may help prompt the teacher's awareness of the meanings contained within the text, and suggest a possible approach to the content via a particular point of entry into the narrative. '*Where's My Teddy?* is potentially packed with learning potential! The teacher could consider *what if. . . .*

- *the story never happened?* – an influential character succeeds in challenging the protagonist at a key moment, and so alters the course of events. For example: 'friends' of Eddy (the children in role) advise him (teacher-in-role) on the viability of going back into the woods to look for his teddy, and consider an alternative solution.
- *the story is evidence?* – key characters are involved in a similar situation but a new context. For example: Eddy (teacher-in-role) has lost his teddy this time at the beach, and asks his friends (children in role) to help him. What do they suggest in the light of what happened last time he went off to look for something on his own?
- *the story happened in the past?* – implications of the outcome of the original story are explored. For example: Eddy (teacher-in-role) is now very careful over his teddy, and one day trusts his friends (children in role) to look after it while he nips out . . . can they keep it safe, even if a caller at the door (assistant in role or teacher in a clear switch of role) tries to persuade them to hand it over?
- *the story is happening elsewhere?* – taking a sideways step – the soap opera genre – to explore a plausible parallel scene to the main story. For example: Eddy's Mum

(teacher-in-role) is very worried because he is missing, and asks other villagers (children in role) for help.

- *the story will happen in the future?* – a key moment is explored that logically could have occurred before the story as known. For example: The teddy bear's picnic in the woods has to be abandoned (why?), causing Eddy (teacher or assistant in role) and his playgroup friends (children in role) to leave in a hurry.

There may be value in 'living through' events in chronological sequence, sticking more closely to the familiar storyline, but pausing to explore tensions at certain key moments in the narrative. This can be a useful approach for teachers beginning in drama, to dip into the narrative in order to 'unpack' an embedded meaning, but in the context of a single scene. This may be achieved by:

- *Meeting a character at a point in the story* – for example, the giant bear (teacher-in-role) comes across some people (children in role) having a teddy bear's picnic in the woods: the bear is upset because he has no friends, everyone is always scared of him because he's big and looks frightening . . . and to top it all, he's lost his teddy, so he can't even join in their fun . . . Improvise the scene and come to some positive resolution.

- *Exploring a significant theme or illustration in depth* – for example, re-creating the final image of Eddy still looking terrified, but now tucked up in bed (played by assistant in role initially, then transferring the role to individual children): what is he thinking? What words could describe his ordeal, his expression? 'Hot-seat' individual children and 'thought track' using paper 'thinks bubbles', and discuss what could help Eddy feel better.

- *Turning tables unexpectedly on the expected course of events* – for example, improvise the story (children in role as a collective Eddy) to the teacher's narration, following the storybook faithfully, but on his return home, Eddy is confronted by his mum (teacher-in-role), who shows a mixture of reactions – angry, relieved, upset. Using freeze-frame and transferring the role to an assistant, analyse with the group her range of expressions and discuss why she should show this mixture of emotions.

- *Living through the story in parallel, experiencing the same tensions as the main characters* – for example, Eddy (teacher-in-role) takes his friends (children in role) with him into the woods to look for his teddy; their quest requires them to tiptoe in turn past a sleeping creature (assistant in role) who then wakes up and chases the individual. Devise a Prescribed Drama Structure that hinges on a 'beat the bogeyman' principle.

- *Edging along one step ahead of the story* – for example, pausing a (first) reading of the story just at the moment where something had made Eddy 'stop quite still': what (else) could it be? Improvise what happens next, with the teacher and group all being a collective Eddy, and an assistant member of staff playing any additional characters . . . out of role, then return to the original story; discuss how the two versions differ.

- *Continuing the story* – for example, it is now the next morning, and Eddy (assistant in role) has had such a terrible night's sleep, that he won't wake up and will be late for school: Eddy's Mum (teacher-in-role) enlists the help of Eddy's friends. Devise a PDS involving the children carrying out part of his morning routine (for example, washing his face, brushing his hair), building in a 'look out behind you!' game, as Eddy falls back asleep behind his Mum's back at the end of each child's turn.

- *Meeting a character afterwards* – for example, after a reading of the story, the group have a chance to interview one of the characters. Teacher-in-role as either the Bear or Eddy can present that character's perspective on the narrative, answering questions from the children and leading discussion around to their advice for the future (for example, how can the Bear make friends? How can Eddy ensure he stays safe?).

Drama and text

Drama can also support children's understanding of narrative in another way: it may be used to show how the written word can convey meaning, and also to develop an awareness and understanding of different layers of meaning in a text (QCA 2001b). This relationship between drama and text may be of crucial significance for certain children with autism, who are renowned for their hyperlexia: that is, possessing sufficient skill to read fluently (often self-taught, having 'cracked the code') yet being unable to understand the meanings contained in the narrative sufficiently to answer simple questions about what they have just read.

Clearly, development in children's speaking and listening skills will have a direct influence on their literacy skills and their ability to use these skills meaningfully to create improvised or rehearsed scripts. Equally, drama may provide a meaningful context in which to write in a particular style or for a particular purpose, or to read and interpret visual and written material, recognising that sounds and words can relate to people, situations, actions and objects (QCA 2001b). For example, the children could help Mrs Pig to match written labels to her pictorial jobs diary. At a more sophisticated level, in role as the gardeners, they could write a letter (individually or as a group, handwritten themselves or by an adult scribe, or computer generated text) protesting about the proposed development plans for Monet's garden, with the written word supported as appropriate by objects, pictures or symbols. What would be the best way of expressing this? Angrily? Politely? Persuasively?

Drama offers opportunities for children with autism to develop an active response to literature, and to identify and describe characters, events, settings and emotions in fiction, and to reflect on their inherent meaning (QCA 2001b). The following example illustrates some direct ways of using an existing text (pictorial and/or written) to enable children to create their own dialogue, and possibly a written play script, in order to express meaning and communicate their thoughts, ideas, feelings and experiences. It will be more appropriate for those children with autism who have achieved at least a stage of symbolic/sociodramatic play development. Their ability as playwrights will be enhanced through their own participation in classroom drama, and their growing awareness and appreciation of the mental states of others.

At first, dialogue may need to be developed within the whole group: imitating and experimenting in shared writing through demonstration, with the teacher (or assistant) scribing and supporting composition. It may be more appropriate initially for the teacher and assistant in role to take the parts of the characters, but gradually to work towards exchange of roles with the children. The text can be extended as dialogue develops, so that the direct relationship between action and the spoken and/or written word is seen. Alternatively – or additionally – the emerging play script may be recorded as a pictorial story board (photographs or drawings), on audio or video tape, as well as a written text.

The following pointers are based on support materials for the National Literacy Strategy (DfES 2001a and 2001b). Examples illustrate how the familiar version of *Where's My Teddy?* could be dramatised, although through classroom drama developed from the original narrative, a new plot structure could well have emerged – and this could become an equally viable play script. Exploring implict meanings in the story beforehand through classroom drama will enable children with autism to gain insights and understanding to bring to a subsequent dramatisation. This will afford them meaningful engagement with the narrative, rather than a superficial reenactment of the sequence of events.

To develop a strong narrative structure, 'playwrights' will need to consider:

- what the speaker and listener do;
- what else is happening;
- the contribution of the setting;
- clarity in the way they communicate meaning:
  - keeping dialogue succinct,
  - developing a few well defined characters (through their mannerisms, actions and speech),
  - ensuring movement is economical and significant,
  - keeping the story idea simple (*little boy loses his teddy and goes back to look for it*),
  - planning a simple plot structure – for example:

boy in woods – finds giant teddy – meets real bear with his teddy – they exchange teddies – home safe

- how the story will progress:
  - triggers that spur key moments (*a sound of sobbing is heard*),
  - change of place (*back at home*),
  - change of time (*later that evening*),
  - change of character (*a gigantic Bear appears*),
  - change of event (*Eddy suddenly spots an enormous teddy*),
  - change of speaker ('*A boy!' yelled the Bear*).

- possible use of a narrator:
  - as a detached observer to set the scene ('*it was late afternoon – Eddy was looking for his lost teddy*'),
  - to move the action forward ('*suddenly Eddy heard a strange noise*'),
  - describing characters' actions as they are performed ('*the gigantic bear crashed his way through the trees*'),
  - offering opinion or comment on the action ('*Eddy had never seen such a large bear before*').

- how to create individual characters by:
  - what they say,
  - how they say it,   } influenced by the character's 'type' (bossy, etc) and 'feelings' (angry, sad, happy, etc), and how they *change* as a result of what happens to them
  - what they actually do,
  - other characters' responses to them (verbal and/or non-verbal),
  - a narrator's comments.

- possible ways to distinguish the end of the play by:
  - clearly showing the character(s)' feelings,
  - reflecting on events (providing a moral) – spoken by a character or narrator,
  - looking to the future,
  - referring to an influential moment from the story,
  - making a link with the beginning of the play, to indicate how the character(s) have changed.

In this way, children with autism may learn to take pleasure in writing for its own sake, and use different styles for a range of purposes with growing confidence. They should be supported in planning, drafting and editing, as necessary, harnessing the meaningful context (and their motivation!) to work on spelling, punctuation, handwriting and presentation skills, and attending to grammar, sentence structure and choice of words. The 'playwrights' should also be shown how to write succinct stage directions for the actions and behaviour of the characters. The following activities may seem beyond the abilities of many children with autism. However, the spectrum is broad, and the potential of certain children may at present lie deceptively dormant and untapped.

Example: 'The Iron Man' (by Ted Hughes)

This classic children's story relates the sudden emergence from the earth of a giant Iron Man, and the responses of the inhabitants of a coastal community. He causes major disruption, and strategies are put in place to deal with him, which prove temporarily effective, and lull everyone into a false sense of security. However, the Iron Man re-emerges, and it takes the wit of a young boy, Hogarth, to find a more humane solution.

The story then moves on, and the whole world is in imminent danger from what seems to be a star from outer space on collision course with planet Earth. It turns out to be a terrifying space-bat-angel-dragon, who proves impossible to placate, and insuperable by any aggressive means of dealing with him. Hogarth pleads with the Iron Man for help; he obliges, and, now as champion of Earth, he challenges the dragon to a test of strength. The dragon succumbs, and as penance, is required to return to Orion, and provide peaceful music for the benefit of the world.

Improvisation into script

Two people improvise a scene in a house (they need to have decided who they are, their relationship to one another, which room and where in the space they are positioned); a third enters with a problem that the Iron Man has caused – reactions of the other two? Develop the scenes immediately before and after this pivotal scene, then create a storyboard as a script (pictorial and/or written).

Embedding dialogue

A key line from the story is given to the children (individually or in groups) to be expanded either side to script a short scene. For example *'An Iron Man, an Iron Man, a giant!'* The children have to work out who says this line and to whom, and what was happening immediately beforehand and then afterwards. What is the response of neighbours/family/farmers?

Creating a storyboard from an extract

Teacher selects a couple of lines of dialogue from the text. For example, *'Enough, enough, enough!' . . . 'No, no, I feel like going on. We've only had two each'.* Children (in groups) decide who could say these two lines and create a context (not necessarily connected with 'The Iron Man' at all – it could be a completely different context). They then add a few lines either side of this pivotal line, to create a short scene. This script could be passed to others to perform.

Illustration as a stimulus for soundscape/poetry
Teacher shows the group an image (for example, of The Iron Man's hand emerging through the ground to disrupt a family picnic), and invites the children to create sounds to go with the picture. Orchestrate, and possibly tape or write down to create a storyboard in sound.

Illustration as a stimulus for a rehearsed improvisation/script
Create a frozen image from an illustration and bring to life (for example, the image of a woman reading a newspaper over a man's shoulder). Children script dialogue, possibly using speech/thinks bubbles, and devise scenes (storyboard) immediately before/afterwards.

Text as a stimulus for a rehearsed improvisation/script
A prescribed line is to be a narrated lead into an ensuing scene. For example, *'The furious farmers began to shout... they would have to do something'.* Children improvise and/or script, and devise an ensuing scene to illustrate what the farmers did. This can be made into a pictorial storyboard, and/or script with brief dialogue and stage directions.

Text as ending
Children to create a scene for which a short prescribed piece of text provides the final lines; for example, *'so there they left him ... It was an Iron Man's heaven. The farmers went back to their farms.'* Children improvise and/or script, adding stage directions for others to perform.

Players with a purpose

The dynamic quality of play and drama make experiences stimulating, affirming and memorable. Play-drama intervention targets the fundamental difficulty in affective functioning experienced by children with autism, which may lead to an enhanced sense of self and receptiveness to others, and improvement in communication and social interaction. Developing and extending their social play by exploring and reflecting on analogous content in drama may put children with autism in touch with their feeling responses to human experiences and help them consider those of others. They may be led to a better understanding of their social world and how to solve some of life's daily problems. Gaining greater control and understanding of their feeling responses, and of the narrative form, may further enrich their life experience, and enable them to find a growing sense of fulfilment in making and sharing meanings in and through drama.

Postscript: Implications for play in practice

Signatories from almost every country across the world have subscribed to the United Nations Convention on the Rights of the Child. In Article 31 of this convention, these countries have agreed to ' . . . recognize the right of the child to engage in play . . . appropriate to the age of the child . . . ' (United Nations High Commissioner for Human Rights 1990).

To allow children with autism to be deprived of the opportunities that exist within play and drama is in opposition to educational guidance and morally unacceptable. By using a relevant and structured approach through play-drama intervention, children with autism *can* learn to open the door and explore the world outside. This book has provided a framework that should assist teachers, parents, therapists and psychologists to allow children with autism and autistic spectrum disorders the right to play, the right to develop their latent potential.

This chapter considers implications for realising these grand aims through play-drama intervention. Curricular issues are discussed, in order to confirm the validity of play and drama as an entitlement within current provision and statutory contexts. A concluding rationale for play-drama intervention is presented, as an integrating and viable way forward for children with autism.

Play and drama in the curriculum

Learning through play is enshrined in the guidance for the Foundation stage curriculum for the early years: 'Well-planned play, both indoors and outdoors, is a key way in which young children learn with enjoyment and challenge' (QCA 2000: 25).

Curriculum guidance recognises the crucial role of the practitioner in:

- planning and resourcing a challenging environment;

- supporting children's learning through planned play activity;
- extending and supporting children's spontaneous play;
- extending and developing children's language and communication in their play.

(QCA 2000: 25)

'Through play, in a secure environment with effective adult support, children can:

- explore, develop and represent learning experiences that help them make sense of the world;
- practise and build up ideas, concepts and skills;
- learn how to control impulses and understand the need for rules;
- be alone, be alongside others or cooperate as they talk or rehearse their feelings;
- take risks and make mistakes;
- think creatively and imaginatively;
- communicate with others as they investigate or solve problems;
- express fears or relive anxious experiences in controlled and safe situations'.

(QCA 2000: 25)

This book has demonstrated the significance of these statements in play-drama intervention and has presented a means to realise these aspirations in relation to children with autism. In the early years, play also has particular curricular status within the area of learning for Creative Development (QCA 2000), which explicitly identifies the promotion of role play and imaginative play. As children mature, their play becomes transformed. It is possible, however, to track an exploratory, investigative approach through many areas within National Curriculum documentation across the Key Stages.

Of all subjects, drama arguably harnesses play the most overtly – it is gratifying therefore, that its status is compulsory now, within the core subject of English (DfEE 1999). Uses of drama can be widespread across the curriculum, as Chapter 5 has demonstrated, not just restricted to timetabled opportunities within English. Drama is a challenging way to teach, though the rewards are bountiful, for both teacher and child. In recognition of some of the particular difficulties the teacher faces in drama, some pointers to support practice are offered in Appendix C.

As well as discrete foundation subjects such as history and geography, play-drama intervention can be used to develop the underlying key and thinking skills that are required to understand other subjects: for example, communication, working with others, improving own learning and performance, and problem solving. Thinking skills for children with learning difficulties may include: the coordination of the use of senses (movement and vision, touch and taste), predicting and anticipating, remembering (by picturing, verbal rehearsal and clustering), the understanding of cause and effect, linking objects, events and experiences and thinking creatively and imaginatively – through play and experimentation, through the discovery and application of new connections and ideas and through active exploration (based on QCA 2001a).

The value of play-drama intervention for children with autism can be summarised as follows:

- By engaging in flexible thinking processes, play and drama help to integrate perceptual, narrative and affective representations and encourage coherence.
- Play and drama develop fluidity and fluency in the thinking process, and assist in the development of alternative strategies and a better understanding of ambiguity.
- By the repeated practice of examining concepts through play and drama, connections in the brain are strengthened and become more effective.
- Play and drama assist in planning, problem solving, simulation and social learning by engaging the child in narrative thought.
- Play and drama provide a framework that allows emotional engagement with others and supports social understanding through shared meanings.
- Play and drama directly explore how social constructs are created, and how to influence others effectively.

All these features are important in developing social understanding and an associated improvement in social interaction skills, communication and greater flexibility of thought and action. Rather than considering there to be a triad of *impairments* could be perceived based on impoverished functioning, instead a triad of *competencies* could be perceived that are released through play and drama. This enables children with autism to explore potential that they already have but do not use. Building upon these latent skills enables children with autism to develop higher competencies within the triad, so that they may function more effectively within a social world.

Play-drama intervention: a rationale

Despite the potential that play and drama have to offer the child with autism, their use has been under-represented in practice and in research. In the preceding chapters, a framework has emerged that supports the teaching of play and drama for children with autism. Combining these approaches is an original position and offers a new way of educating children with autism by integrating their thinking and feeling processes within carefully paced, structured contexts. At the core of play-drama intervention lies the premise that children with autism have a latent potential to learn how to use their imagination and develop their understanding of narrative – this can be explicitly taught using play and drama.

Play-drama intervention requires children to think creatively – this is the same flexibility of mind that is impaired in autism. Using the imagination opens opportunities for exploring make-believe and narrative, and at the same time, the possibility of strengthening the neural structures involved. A range of solitary and social play contexts have been described, and also models for developing prescribed and more open-ended drama. These form a coherent framework that spans different stages of development, and which can be used with children across the age range and also in adult teaching provision.

The use of developmentally appropriate structures will facilitate the progress of many children with autism who are at present not able to use play and drama. It is possible to engage children with autism in pretend play and involve them in drama that challenges their make-believe and extends their narrative understanding. The importance of social contexts has been demonstrated; additionally, play and drama experiences need to be meaningful to the interests and emotional engagement of the child. Although the authors have first-hand experience of rapid progress in several children with autism, most are likely to make slow but steady progress in these areas.

As play-drama intervention appeals to both the cognitive strengths and the essential playfulness of children with autism, they may feel energised and liberated to make creative choices and decisions within carefully constructed parameters. Over time, as boundaries are extended, children with autism may develop an ability to think more laterally in situations and with greater flexibility, and understand better their own behaviour and that of others, so building an enhanced understanding of a social world.

Play-drama intervention offers a powerful, integrating way forward for children with autism, that addresses the learning needs of the whole person. Rather than characterising the child with autism by a 'triad of impairments', we use play and drama to enable him or her to be seen as a contributing member of society, characterised instead by a potential 'triad of competencies': enhanced creativity, sensitivity and communication . . . .Through play-drama intervention, it is possible to bring the worlds (real and imaginary) of those with and without autism closer together.

We'd like to leave the last word with Sam, the eldest son of one of the authors. At the age of ten, he demonstrated remarkable insights, and totally captured the essence of this book! Commenting on life with his brother who has autism, he offered professionals this advice:

> Be patient. If you're trying to do something with them, stay calm and relaxed. Keep at it. Try to make what you're doing sound interesting. Make up games about the things they like. So if you're trying to teach them to count to 3, then say 'Look Jesse, Postman Pat has 1, 2, 3 letters to post: Jesse, put the letters in door number three!' . . . Make it about them, and then they'll pay attention.

Appendix A: Practical strategies for teaching play

It is helpful to have a starting point in planning structured opportunities for teaching play to children with autism. There follows a series of examples for particular play structures described in Chapter 3, suitable for children at different stages of their play development. The activities are intended to stimulate teachers to adapt ideas to the needs and interests of their children rather than being a list of definitive teaching methods. Additional information is noted within each play structure to indicate suggested group size, play abilities of the children, and also level of affect.

Rationale – This statement indicates why the particular narrative was chosen for the activity and the materials used. Some activities are designed to use materials that have a high level of interest to many children with autism. Other activities use materials that are designed to facilitate symbolic play because they have features that are suggestive of potential symbolic transformations that would sit well in a particular narrative. Further activities often work because they have an inherent affective interest to children with autism.

Affect – Some of the strategies suggest high or low levels of affect. High affect would indicate the teacher uses or encourages moderately high levels of excitement and may use a range of pronounced or exaggerated expressions of emotion. In the low affect strategies, teachers should aim to keep the activity on an 'even keel' and allow the child to focus on the structure of the activity. Teachers should make critical judgements in the use of affect: what works for one child may have an opposite effect on another.

Causal significance – Each play structure suggests a 'causal significance' for the activity. This allows the teacher to emphasise particular aspects, in order to highlight explicitly to the child(ren) the underlying patterns for the sequence of activities – how key moments or events connect to one another – and so encourage a greater sense of coherence (meaning) for the child.

Play stage – Guidance is offered in identifying appropriate activities, although many could be easily extended or modified to include children with higher or lower play abilities. The following abbreviations are used:

- Sens for Sensori-motor
- Rel for Relational
- Func for Functional
- Sym for Symbolic play
- Soc for Sociodramatic.

Play Structure 1: Expansion

Pots of Food

Play Structure 1
Play stage — Expansion / Sens/Rel
Individual/group — Individual
Affective level — Low

Rationale This activity takes pans and lids of different sizes. Each pan is filled with different objects.

Materials Pans and lids, plastic food, cuddly toys, plastic balls, cling film, disc shaped counters, wooden blocks and sticky tape.

Activity The child is given a pan to play with. The pan contains items of plastic food. When this is disregarded, the child is offered another pan. This one is filled with cuddly toys. As this is dispensed with the child is offered a third pan this time containing plastic balls and wrapped in cling film before the lid is put on. The fourth pan contains large disc shaped counters. The final pan is filled with wooden blocks and the lid is sealed on with lots of sticky tape.

Extension Plastic fruit juice bottles may be filled with an assortment of objects and handed to the child. The teacher sensitively shows interest in the child's actions with the bottles and demonstrates enthusiasm at the contents where this is appropriate.

Causal significance *Objects that look the same may contain items that you have seen before or they may contain something different. This may make you/us pleased or it may not.*

Coloured Buckets

Play Structure 1
Play stage — Expansion / Sens/Rel
Individual/group — Individual
Affective level — Low to moderate

Rationale Extending possibilities for children who enjoy putting objects in containers.

Materials A number of brightly coloured buckets and objects of different sizes, weights, textures, colours and sounds.

Activity The child is allowed to put objects in a bucket and empty the bucket afterwards. The child is offered a variety of objects. The teacher offers a choice of two objects. The teacher shows pleasure in the choice that the child has taken and again when it is removed from the bucket.

Extension Use boxes with lids instead of buckets. Show pleasure and disgust at the choice of object.

Causal significance *The teacher shows an interest in the same object as the child. The teacher demonstrates affect in expressions that are judged to stimulate the child's interest in the objects. The teacher also shows positive affect at the process that the child is engaged in by showing pleasure at the choice, insertion and removal of the object from the bucket.*

Basketball

Play Structure 1	Expansion
Play stage	Sens/Rel
Individual/group	Individual
Affective level	Low to moderate

Rationale Sometimes children with autism can spend long periods of development involved in the same interests and using the same routines. This activity attempts to extend a throwing routine by involving another person in the game.

Materials A ball-pool and a large basket.

Activity The child is sitting in the ball-pool. He or she constantly throws balls across the pool for the entire stay in the pool. The teacher sits in the pool or moves around its edge. As the child throws a ball the teacher tries to catch it in a large basket. If the teacher is successful, he or she cheers, if not, despairs 'Oh dear'.

Extension Instead of a basket, the teacher uses a large sound-making instrument such as a large tambourine. The teacher attempts to hold this up to the balls as they are thrown. If a ball hits the tambourine, the teacher makes additional sweeping movements and rattling sounds in celebration of the success.

Causal significance *My actions can cause an entertaining response in others.*

Cave paintings

Play Structure 1	Expansion
Play stage	Sens/Rel
Individual/group	Individual
Affective level	Low

Rationale This activity is designed for children who like small spaces and sometimes like a quiet place on their own. Everyday materials are used to construct the cave, which may start to build an idea that objects can be used in different ways. It is important that the materials are changed regularly to reduce reliance on their sameness.

Materials A variety of materials and textures that can be safely used in a relatively unsupervised setting, and children's paintings.

Activity A cave is made from a cupboard, large cardboard box or a sheet tied and draped over a table. The cave is decorated with fabric squares, children's paintings or articles of clothing that are hung along the walls. Different textures are used for flooring; spiral shaped mobiles are constructed from scrap materials and hung from the ceiling. A door is made by hanging fabric or paper strips over a curtain wire. Each night the materials are changed slightly so that the combination of materials is never the same.

Extension The teacher or another child may be tolerated inside the cave or can take an interest in its contents.

The child is encouraged to make choices about which materials to introduce and to be involved in adding them to the cave.

Different constructions may be made that incorporate these ideas such as a rabbit burrow, an igloo, a space rocket or a submarine.

Causal significance *The materials frequently change but the underlying concept of a 'cave' remains constant.*

Play Structure 2: Modelled Routines

Washing Day			
	Play Structure 2	Modelled Routines	
	Play stage	Rel/Func	
	Individual/group	Either	
	Affective level	Any	
Rationale	This routine teaches the children some of the sequences involved in playing with clothes.		
Materials	A cardboard box, assorted clothing, length of string and clothes pegs.		
Activity	The activity begins by trying on clothing from the dressing up box. All the children may wear whatever they can find. The teacher then announces that it is Washing Day and all the dressing up clothes must be washed. The children remove the clothes and place them in the cardboard box. The children may add jugs of pretend water if preferred and stir round the clothes by turning the box. The teacher may wish to set a stop-clock or egg-timer with a buzzer to indicate the wash cycle is over. When the washing is ready, the children may remove an item of clothing and hang it on the washing line that is tied between two pieces of solid furniture. When the washing is dry the children may pack it away or decide to wear it once more.		
Extension	The children dress a doll or teddy bear to go out for a walk and then get it ready for bath and bed.		
Causal significance	*I want to wear that item of clothing. She wants to wear something else. I want to peg out this scarf. She wants to peg out that hat. Sometimes we will want the same things and other times we will not.*		

Crashing Aeroplanes			
	Play Structure 2	Modelled Routines	
	Play stage	Rel/Func	
	Individual/group	Either	
	Affective level	Any	
Rationale	This routine is often attractive because of the crashing aeroplanes. It is designed to teach aeroplane flying skills and crashing routines.		
Materials	A variety of toy aeroplanes and small world items.		
Activity	The teacher pretends that a series of aeroplanes are taking off by making thunderous sounds at lift off. The aeroplanes fly round in a big circle and then either land carefully or crash noisily into a tree, house or any stationary object. The child may be offered alternate aeroplanes or left alone with a selection following the demonstration.		
Extension	Use aeroplanes that can fit people in and incorporate this as an extra part of the routine. Attach an elastic band to the table and propel the aeroplanes onto the runway on the ground.		
Causal significance	*You can watch me turn a toy into an animated aeroplane. I can watch you do exciting things with it as well. Now watch this!*		

Puppet Hide

Play Structure 2	Modelled Routines
Play stage	Rel/Func
Individual/group	Either
Affective level	Any

Rationale
This is a puppet version of hide and seek or peek-a-boo. It is designed to teach the play routine of hide and surprise.

Materials
Two friendly looking hand-puppets and two cardboard boxes with doors cut out and windows drawn on the back of the house partially removed to allow easy puppet access.

Activity
In a house made from a large cardboard box a puppet is hiding. The other puppet looks in each house to discover where the first puppet is hiding. When the first puppet is found, both puppets make excited giggling sounds and jump up and down. The child is offered the use of the searching puppet at first and eventually both puppets.

Extension
A different puppet is substituted into the house without the child seeing.

Causal significance
My puppet is looking for the other one. He doesn't know where it is. When he finds it, we will be very excited. If my puppet looks in the wrong place, we will be disappointed. You and I are both attending to the puppets and our reactions may or may not be the same.

Rowing Boats

Play Structure 2	Modelled Routines
Play stage	Rel/Func/Sym
Individual/group	Either
Affective level	Any

Rationale
This activity aims to teach the skills required for rowing boats and for some children pretending to find it hard work and be tired.

Materials
A large cardboard box.

Activity
The teacher sits in a large cardboard box and pretends to row using two large oars. The teacher can use simple language to describe the journey such as 'boat ... oars ... water ... waves'. After a few moments the teacher tires and slows down saying 'oh tired, hard work'. The teacher stops rowing and looks over his or her shoulder before restarting.

Extension
Pretend a shark is coming to eat the boat each time the child becomes tired.

Place a large blue sheet under the box. Each time the child slows down the sheet is wafted to make big waves and the child must row very quickly once more.

For children capable of symbolic play, the boat can convert into a car as it reaches land. The child swaps imaginary oars for a steering wheel and gear stick and the box becomes a car. The child then arrives at the airport and the steering wheel becomes aeroplane wings as the child flies back to the water.

We can all join in together in an imaginary ocean ...cause we all agreed that the sea was there. Thoughts in ...eads can be shared and mutually acted upon as long ...mmunicate this to each other.

Play Structure 3: Narrative

Walk on the Wild Side

Play Structure 3	Narrative
Play stage	Func
Individual/group	Small group
Affective level	Moderate

Rationale
This activity uses a sequence of visual prompts, imitation and group momentum to create a narrative suitable for children with pre-symbolic play.

Materials
Lots and lots of assorted clothing and footwear.

Activity
While the children are out on a pretend walk around the room the weather changes rapidly. The teacher holds up a picture of the new weather conditions and says 'Oh dear it is raining . . . put on your coats'. Each child is given a coat to put on. The group continues once more around the room. The teacher stops and says 'Oh no it is raining harder . . . come under my umbrella'. The group shelters from the rain and resumes walking together under the umbrella. On the third circuit the teacher stops once more and holds up a picture of windy weather saying 'Goodness me . . . it's very windy'. The group huddles under the umbrella and pushes it into the wind as the resume their walk is resumed. The next time the teacher stops, he or she reports is snowing and issues warm hats for all the walkers. On the final circuit of the room, the group has reached the sea and the weather is sunny and warm. The teacher shows the children a picture of sunshine and tells them to take off their shoes and socks so they can paddle in the water.

Extension
Familiar stories such as 'We're going on a bear hunt' provide wonderful extensions to this type of narrative.

Causal significance
We are all joining in with imaginative pretence. We all agree to behave as if the weather is changing.

When the weather changes, what do we do? When it was raining, which ones of these did you use? When she wore the woolly hat, what was the weather doing? When you wore the sunglasses, what was the weather doing?

Three Little Pigs

Play Structure 3	Narrative
Play stage	Func/Early sym
Individual/group	Either
Affective level	Moderate to high

Rationale
Many children are familiar with this story. This familiarity provides a narrative structure for this play activity.

Materials
A cardboard box, a pig and a wolf.

Activity
The teacher acts as narrator and shows the children the pictures in the storybook. As the story proceeds, the teacher uses a single cardboard box as each of the houses. The pig must act as each of the three little pigs and the wolf can be played by any dog-like toy. The climax of the story is the pigs' revenge on the wolf who scorches his tail. This should be accompanied by lots of excitement and yelping from the wolf as he scampers away. The children can then be offered the use of the materials to play.

Extension
This type of activity works with many traditional stories, such as 'Jack and the Beanstalk', 'Red Riding Hood' or 'Goldilocks and the Three Bears'. The teacher should give consideration to the level of representational materials required by the children and the level of symbolism that would be required.

Causal significance
The pigs know the wolf is on the roof but the wolf does not know that the pigs have lit a fire.

Who Has Taken Fox's Breakfast?

Play Structure 3		Narrative
Play stage		Func/Sym
Individual/group		Either
Affective level		Moderate to high

Rationale
This activity develops a simple narrative about taking things from others.

Materials
Several animal hand-puppets or other animal toys and plastic food.

Activity
Fox is asleep in his lair (under a table) and wakes up hungry. He collects the food he wants for his breakfast and sits down to eat. Unfortunately Fox is still sleepy and puts his head down for a nap. While he snores loudly, a child is given another animal puppet and encouraged to take an apple from Fox. When this has gone, Fox wakes up to discover some of his dinner is missing and is unbelievably outraged, 'Who has taken my apple? Is it you? Is it you?' Exhausted by his exertions, Fox settles back down for a nap, warning all nearby creatures, 'I'm going to sleep, nobody must take my breakfast!' Each time a different animal takes an item of food, Fox wakes and makes his discontent known. The activity can be repeated with different children taking the role of Fox.

Extension
When all the food is removed the animals may decide to take pity on Fox and give back all the food.

Fox may decide to lay a trap by putting the food under a large box that is propped up by a stick.

For children who are working at a higher symbolic level, Fox could sleep through the whole episode while his breakfast is boiling in a large pan. Does Fox know that all his food has gone? Where does Fox think his food is?

Causal significance
Fox does not know that his food has been taken because he was asleep. The other puppet wanted Fox's food, Fox wanted his food. Fox was upset when his food was taken.

Dolly Drops the Shopping

Play Structure 3		Narrative
Play stage		Func/Sym
Individual/group		Either
Affective level		Moderate

Rationale
This activity aims to create an everyday narrative about shopping with an unfortunate twist.

Materials
A doll, a small bag, a small purse and food items.

Activity
On the way home from the supermarket, dolly's shopping bag tears and the contents fall out. She does not notice that her bag is getting lighter. The children in the room very kindly recover the lost shopping and return it to dolly as she walks the long journey back to her home. Dolly is very grateful and thanks each child as they give her the lost possessions.

Extension
The contents of Dolly's bag cause chaos as the car that is trying to travel up the same street keeps bumping into her shopping on the road. Dolly is most apologetic and repeatedly says 'Sorry' to the car driver.

Causal significance
Dolly doesn't know that her food is missing because she didn't see it fall out of her bag. The children (or the car driver) did see the food and responded accordingly.

Dolly did not want to lose her food. The children wanted her to get her food back. Dolly was very pleased and communicated this to the children.

Play Structure 4 : Flexible Narrative

Storyboard Adventure	
Play Structure 4	Flexible Narrative
Play stage	Func/Sym
Individual/group	Group
Affective level	Moderate
Rationale	The narrative is structured using a storyboard to provide a visual prompt and predictability to the process, but with developing flexibility.
Materials	A series of cotton sheets, items of large furniture and an assortment of fabric pieces and dressing up clothes.
Activity	The children look at a story about a journey and then modify it so that the main characters meet a series of obstacles or people that can help on their journey. A grid is drawn on a large sheet of card and a picture is drawn into each square on the grid to represent the sequence of obstacles.

The sheets are draped over tables and chairs to represent each obstacle. This may then be a high mountain, a dark cave or the lair of a toothy crocodile. One child dresses as an inhabitant of this setting by being wrapped in a piece of cloth, fun-fur or clothing. The main characters are reminded of their journey by referring to the storyboard and set off on their adventure and encounter their first obstacle. After their encounter, the children re-assemble and refer back to the storyboard and plan the next leg of their journey. |
| Causal significance | *What is inside the cave? What is hiding behind the mountain?*

I can remember what the map showed us ... it showed a sleeping troll in the cave ... we must be very quiet and tiptoe past. |

Frightened Monster	
Play Structure 4	
Play stage	
Individual/group	Gr...
Affective level	High
Rationale	This fifteen minute activity aims to children using a simple routine of appro... monster, but to do so dynamically as this us... a very loose narrative.
Materials	A cotton sheet or square of brightly coloured fabric.
Activity	The teacher drapes the sheet over his or her head and tells a story (better to use a narrator) about being a monster who is frightened of everything and everyone. Each time the children move towards the monster, it must respond by trembling visibly or running away in panic, only to return to the children. The children can then try wearing the sheet and playing the Frightened Monster.
Extension	The narrator can change the narrative by telling the children they must be quiet when the monster comes back, or they must be kind to the monster and make him a cup of tea. The monster can of course be frightening and the children pretend to be scared (care needs to be taken to prevent the children becoming over-excited in this version).
Causal significance	*I like the monster, it makes me smile. The monster does not feel the same as I do. I must be sensitive to the monster's feelings if it is to stay.*

Train Disaster

Play Structure 4	Flexible Narrative
Play stage	Func /Sym
Individual/group	Individual
Affective level	Moderate to High

Rationale
This activity might build upon earlier narrative forms about train journeys. In this version the child is asked to take additional unexpected events into account and take pleasure in overcoming these (simple) problems.

Materials
Wooden or plastic train track and trains, plastic animals and junk materials.

Activity
A circular train track is laid out on the floor and a train engine and carriages depart on their regular journey. On the second time round, the bridge collapses and the child (as train driver) must rebuild the bridge to continue his journey. On the fourth time round the track, the plastic cow walks on to the train track to eat some grass. What will the train do? On the sixth time round the track, the rails are blocked by a fallen tree (cardboard tube/ pencil). What will the train do?

Extension
Where possible the teacher and child may be able to interact and extend each of these events. The bridge may be repaired with a crane (lying nearby). The possibly injured cow may be repaired by kind Dr Bob who was passing nearby in his ambulance (a box and 'nee-naw' siren sound). The train may be able to fasten a handy rope (piece of string and sticky tape) to the tree and drag it off the line.

Causal significance
The train driver cannot know or see what is on the track until he comes round the bend. Will the train stop in time?

What must you as train driver do to continue on your journey?

Delivery Van

Play Structure 4	Flexible Narrative
Play stage	Rel/Func/Sym
Individual/group	Group
Affective level	Low

Rationale
A straightforward narrative with a little flexibility. The teacher runs a (tabletop) shop and the child drives a delivery van.

Materials
A hoop and a medium sized cardboard box that has been tied onto a waist-belt or cord or a ladies' shoulder bag. A table covered with plastic food and a range of miscellaneous objects.

Activity
The child takes the steering wheel (hoop) of the delivery van and puts on the bag or box. The driver is asked to take a delivery of food to a child in the group. The driver puts the food in his or her bag or box and makes driving noises to the named recipient of the food. When the driver returns, he or she is told to ask the next child what they would like from the shop. The driver asks the child and delivers the item to them. When this is complete another child may wish to be the delivery driver.

Extension
The children may be given plastic pennies to pay for the items they buy.

The van may be delivering blocks to make a huge tower a few at a time or sand for the sandpit.

The van driver sometimes makes a mistake and delivers the incorrect item or the correct item to the wrong customer.

Causal significance
The objects in the shop transfer from the table to the box and then to him or perhaps to me.

The desires of others may or may not be the same as mine.

What did you think that Jim would want? What did Jim ask for? Were you correct?

What did you ask for? What did Jim ask for? What did the van driver give you? Was it the same as you asked for?

Sheepdog

Play Structure 4	Flexible Narrative
Play stage	Func/Sym
Individual/group	Individual
Affective level	Moderate to High

Rationale
In this activity the children pretend to be sheep that have escaped and the teacher must pretend to be the sheepdog that rounds them up.

Materials
Some squares of white fun-fur with a velcro fastening wrapped around the child's clothing will help to support this pretence.

Activity
The teacher shows the children a video of a sheepdog rounding up a stray flock before this activity to ensure that all the children have some narrative basis for this pretence. The teacher may wish to practise some routines prior to the activity to ensure the children also know how to sound and walk like sheep.

The teacher makes a three-sided fence around the children from tables or chairs and asks all the children to be sheep. The sheepdog guards the entrance to the field so that the sheep do not escape. Each time a sheep moves towards the entrance the dog barks, which means, 'Go back'. The dog becomes distracted and all the sheep escape. The dog must chase after each sheep in turn and bark at it to ask it to return to the sheepfold. When all the sheep are returned a different dog can take a turn.

Extension
The sheepdog is very tired and needs a soft bed to lie on. The sheep agree to help the dog and one at a time they find a piece of the dog's bed. The sheep give the dog objects including a blanket, a bone, a pillow and an alarm clock. When the dog has all that he needs, and goes to sleep, the sheep escape once more.

Causal significance
The sheep want to escape, the dog does not want them to.

The dog does not see/know that the sheep have escaped until it wakes. The sheep know that they must wait until the dog sleeps, as it will not otherwise let them pass. Seeing is necessary for knowing.

Transfigurations

Play Structure 4	Flexible Narrative
Play stage	Sym
Individual/group	Either
Affective level	Low

Rationale
An exercise in finding alternatives for those competent at symbolic play.

Materials
A pencil or a box or a piece of rope.

Activity
The children are shown a simple symbolic transformation with one of the objects, e.g. turning the pencil into a spoon to eat porridge with: 'yum, yum, porridge.' The children are asked, 'can you make something different with this pencil?'

Extension
Repeat the exercise using more than one object.

Causal significance
The pictures in your mind can be turned into other things as long as you hold onto the thread of meaning. I cannot understand what is in your head unless you demonstrate the transformation through actions, e.g. this pencil looks a little like a snake because it is long and thin. I can communicate this by making the pencil wiggle like a snake would do.

Play Structure 5: Interactive

Sleeping Tigers

Play Structure 5	Interactive
Play stage	Sym
Individual/group	Small Group
Affective level	Moderate to Low

Rationale This activity is designed to place an individual or small group of children in a quietly exciting state that encourages them to modify a simple sleeping routine.

Materials A quiet comfortable floor area.

Activity The teacher is Mummy (or Daddy) tiger and one or several children are the baby tigers. Mummy tiger wants to sleep but gives no verbal instructions to the cubs. In not speaking the teacher reduces the structure that would otherwise be imposed, and allows this activity to be more interactive. As the cubs lie down quietly, the Mummy tiger purrs reassuringly. If the cubs are too noisy or boisterous, Mummy tiger growls impatiently. (Warning: this activity sometimes results in the cubs jumping on Mummy or Daddy tiger! The teacher should take suitable precautions and preferably have an assistant nearby.)

Extension Mummy tiger's cubs go missing and she calls them back.

The cubs are hungry and are brought back imaginary food.

Causal significance *An understanding of different roles. You must behave like a cub. You sit quietly with Mummy tiger.*

Mummy tiger is tired. The cubs are not tired. The cubs are not tired. Mummy is missing her cubs; she is worried and sad. The cubs are lost and frightened. They must communicate to

Giant Jellyfish

Play Structure 5	Interactive
Play stage	Rel/Func/Sym
Individual/group	Group
Affective level	High

Rationale An exciting and engaging fifteen-minute activity that uses the simplest of narratives in a dynamic interactive structure.

Materials A large cotton sheet or net curtain.

Activity The teacher wears the sheet over his or her head and holds out hands to create a bell shape. Using a slow and gentle bouncing action, the teacher billows the sheet and becomes the Giant Jellyfish. The children become the little fish and must swim away from the jellyfish before they are stung (and possibly sit down). If the jellyfish catches a little fish, it may loosely envelop the fish in the sheet and gently jiggle the little fish before releasing it. The children may then take turns at being the jellyfish.

Extension Use a parachute as the jellyfish. The children must run or swim under the parachute when it billows up and escape as it returns to the floor.

Causal significance *We can all play together. I would / wouldn't like to be caught. He is caught and he is giggling.*

Who will be caught by the jellyfish? Can the jellyfish see me? Perhaps I should swim away?

Kitchen Chaos

Play Structure 5	
Play stage	Interactive
Individual/group	Sym/Soc
Affective level	2 or 3 children
	Moderate

Rationale This activity relies on the chaos that ensues when a dinosaur (or an alternative disruption) wants to help in the kitchen. The teacher needs to quickly step aside.

Materials Plastic crockery and cutlery, plastic food, washing-up bowl, apron, playhouse, table and chairs, dinosaur toy.

Activity A kitchen is made using a table and any suitable kitchen equipment in a playhouse or quiet corner. The table is set with crockery and cutlery and ready for hungry diners. While the cook is preparing food, the second child is given a dinosaur or other toy to help in the kitchen. The dinosaur is very hungry and very, very clumsy. The teacher must withdraw from the scene as soon as the children are engaged with the narrative.

Extension The children are washing up the dishes when an inflatable crocodile wants to swim in the washing-up bowl.

Causal significance *The character that you are playing is following different rules to mine. The cook wants to prepare dinner and the dinosaur wants to eat!*

Bus Driver

Play Structure 5	
Play stage 4	Interactive
Individual/group	Sym/Soc
Affective level	Two children
	Moderate to Low

Rationale This activity requires the teacher to set the scene of a bus journey and the children to be motivated to travel on the bus.

Materials Chairs, child's steering wheel, bus driver's hat, bell/buzzer, two sets of photographs in flip-over book.

Activity A bus is made from six chairs aligned in two adjoining columns. One child is given the bus driver's hat and steering wheel. Both children are given a set of photographs. The photographs show pictures of destinations for the bus. The second child becomes the passenger on the bus and can ask the bus driver to drive to anywhere, including any of the destinations in the photograph book. The teacher must then allow the children to play without further assistance.

Extension The bus may be converted into a taxi taking an injured pedestrian to hospital.

The bus could change into an aeroplane that flies to numerous exotic locations.

Causal significance *The driver may want to go to one destination but must go to the choice of the passenger. Was it the same or were they different?*

The driver does not know which destination the passenger will choose. He or she cannot drive until he or she has this information.

Play Structure 6: Spontaneous

Spider's Dinner

Play Structure 6		Spontaneous
Play stage		Late Func/Soc
Individual/group		Individual or Group
Affective level		Moderate to high

Rationale
Spider toys eat flies and beetles and butterflies and use a piece of string to tie up all kinds of insects. This activity aims to create opportunities for spontaneous play at a functional or symbolic level as the Spider explores the room. The child may work alone or be accompanied by other children. The other children must not dominate the play as this may reduce opportunities for spontaneous play.

Materials
Spider toy, plastic food, animal and people figures and assorted junk materials including several long lengths of string and sticky fixers. The teacher may also wish to prepare a spider's web by threading a loose web through the top of an open cardboard box.

Activity
The child is given a spider toy. The child is told that the spider is hungry and will eat butterflies, houseflies and beetles. The spider does not like moths, mosquitoes or slugs. The teacher might show the child pictures of real insects prior to this if necessary. The spider must take its food back to its web/home first. The room is prepared with an assortment of bottles, boxes and string (insects).

To prevent further influence, the teacher must not give any additional guidance to the child and should walk away to a discrete observational position.

Extension
On a warm summer's day, allow the child to play outside with a plastic fish and a large tray of water that contains possible food items.

Instead of boxes and bottles, children are substituted for insects. The spider should name them, e.g. 'Yum-yum a housefly' or 'Yuck a slug'.

Causal significance
The spider likes some foods and not others. I like different foods from the spider.

The bottles and boxes are not strikingly similar to flies and beetles. This requires the child to use his or her judgement about which ambiguous object is a butterfly and which a moth, which a housefly and which a mosquito, which a beetle and which a slug.

The children do not know their fate until the spider speaks.

What's in the Box?

Play Structure 6		Spontaneous
Play stage 3+/4		Late Func – Sym
Individual/group		Group
Affective level		High

Rationale
In asking the question 'What is in the box?' The teacher opens up possibilities for children to think of things that they would really like (or really dislike) to be in the box. This activity requires the children to be well practised in pretence and capable of understanding some symbolic play.

Materials
A large cardboard box.

Activity
The teacher pretends that there is something in the box. It might be heavy, sweet smelling or scary. The teacher must convey this on his or her face. In this case the teacher rattles the box and says 'What's in the box? S/he reaches in the box to find an imaginary trumpet, and immediately puts it to his or her lips and blares out a tune. The teacher throws away the trumpet and approaches a child. S/he asks 'What's in the box?' Whatever the child replies, the teacher must try and produce from the box to give to the child. If the child says an aeroplane, the teacher drops the box and says 'Phew . . . very heavy!', then gives the aeroplane to the child with open arms and much grunting. The child is allowed to fly around the room in the aeroplane. In anything but a very small group of children, this would have to be a very brief flight. The teacher approaches another child and repeats the question. This child must not choose anything that has already been found in the box and be asked to choose something different.

Extension
With a small group of children any of their ideas can be easily expanded and developed into interactive play structures.

Instead of a box, the teacher holds out her clenched hands and says 'In this hand I have a wriggly snake and in this hand I have a tickly mouse; which would you like?' The teacher offers the appropriately opened hand when the child has chosen the snake or the mouse. Both options are often accompanied by shrieks or giggles.

Causal significance
What did you want to be in the box? Is that what we pretended was in the box? What did you do with it?

The child does not know what is in the teacher's hands. Do you know what is in my hands? It's a . . . . . . !

Magic Wand

Play Structure 6
Play stage — Spontaneous
Individual/group — Highly sym and Soc
Affective level — Individual or Group
Moderate to High

Rationale
This is a potentially exciting activity that relies on the child's understanding of magic, wizards and witches to produce a range of symbolic transformations, modifications and imaginary creations.

Materials
A witch or wizard's cape (square of black cloth tied at two corners), possibly a square of silvery cloth, a black cone-shaped hat and a magic wand (blunt pencil wrapped in silver foil), an assortment of boxes and bottles and large junk materials.

Activity
The child is told that he or she can pretend to use the magic wand but needs to wear the hat and cape. The child can work extra special magic by covering things with the magic silver cloth and tapping it with the wand while saying what it should transform into.

Extension
Other children can sit around the room. The Wizard points the wand and says what the child should turn into.

The teacher acts as the Wizard's Apprentice 'helper'. Sometimes the Wizard transforms objects into things that the Apprentice likes, but sometimes he or she is frightened, disgusted, saddened or excited.

The child could play being the Fairy Godmother in Cinderella. This provides greater narrative structure while allowing sufficient potential for spontaneous symbolic play.

Additional fun could be made from these activities using some computer skills. The teacher photographs each transformation that the child performs with the wand and cloth. Using a copy of PowerPoint (Microsoft Office 97/2000) and a photo-graphics programme, the teacher can make a slide show in which the real object is substituted for the magical object and is accompanied by magical sounds. This can be shown to the child with perhaps some simple explanation of the process involved.

Causal significance
The children watching the Wizard do not know what transformation will come next. Would you do the same or turn it into something different?

The Apprentice doesn't know what the Wizard will do next. S/he wants it to be pleasant. What did s/he think of the wolf? What did s/he think of the chocolate bar?

The Missing Dinner

Play Structure 6
Play stage — Spontaneous
Individual/group — Sym/Soc
Affective level — Individual or Group
Low

Rationale
This activity aims to find a starting point for the child to generate his own pretence by creating an imperative. This activity cannot be used to structure spontaneity if a similar activity has been used previously at a lower level.

Materials
Plastic crockery and cutlery, 3 pieces of plastic food, apron, table and chairs, cuddly toys, plasticine, junk materials.

Activity
The teacher sets the scene with a table set for four cuddly toys and the child is both cook and waiter. Each guest has a plate, knife and fork, but one guest has no plastic food on its plate. The cook has no prepared plastic food left but has a tub of plasticene and a small box of junk materials. The teacher must step out as soon as the child understands the dilemma and must not help with the solution.

Extension
The guests all want dessert after their dinner. What delicious pudding can the cook come up with ?

Causal significance
The guest wants dinner, but there is not enough for them all to have the same.

Why is there not enough? What did the cook do about it? Why did the cook make plasticene food?

Appendix B: Practical strategies for teaching social play

Social play is complex, but will need to be explicitly taught to children with autism. It should be taught *in parallel* to the development of their symbolic understanding, and will need to be perceived as relevant and meaningful. The activities listed below are intended as a starting point to thinking about social play in a practical, developmental way. All the activities would require adapting to the needs, interests and tolerances of each individual child with autism.

Taking play into drama is dependent on establishing a group dynamic. The following activities do not require participation as part of a group, but can focus instead on developing a relationship with a significant adult (or peer). They may also be turned round, so that the child takes the initiative.

Rough and Tumble

Social Play	Two
Play Stage	Any
Group	Individual or Group
Affect	High
Activity	This activity is not for the faint-hearted! The teacher uses a dynamic combination of tickling, chasing, swinging and possibly throwing in a suitable soft and protected environment. The teacher uses repetitive sequences to build prediction. The teacher uses pause, gesture and surprise to accentuate the excitement.

Despite the effectiveness of this technique with even timid, quiet, aloof and touch-intolerant children, we cannot recommend its use beyond the teacher's careful analysis of the physical risks and what child protection issues allow. |
| Evaluative Criteria | Pronounced and meaningful eye contact, requesting behaviour using words, vocalisations, gesture or movement. The child should start to predict repetitive sequences. |
| Causal significance | *The child wants the interaction to continue but is teased by the teacher. When will it happen? The child must read the facial expressions, body postures and vocal intonations of the teacher with uncommon urgency.* |

Incy Wincy Spider

Social Play	One
Play Stage	Any
Group	Individual or Group
Affect	High
Activity	The teacher gently takes the child's wrist and says the words to the rhyme 'Incy Wincy Spider'; the teacher turns his or her fingers into a spider and the creature crawls up the child's arm. The teacher turns his or her fingers to raindrops that drip onto the child's shoulder and the spider tumbles down the child's arm. The teacher indicates the sunshine by drawing a circle with an open hand in the air and the spider crawls back up the child's arm, which finishes with a tickle on the child's shoulder / neck.
Evaluative Criteria	The child should indicate a repeat of the rhyme using words, gesture, eye-contact or by pushing his or her arm towards the teacher. The child starts to predict the final line of the rhyme.
Causal significance	*The teacher and the child are differently engaged in a shared activity. They may start to interchange or exchange roles in this.*

Funny Face

Social Play	Four
Play Stage	Sens/Rel/Func/Sym
Group	Individual or Group
Affect	Moderate to High

Activity

The teacher puts on a red nose and approaches the children. If the children don't respond to the change, the teacher looks directly at the child. Many children will respond to this by trying to remove the nose, others may comment or ask to wear it themselves. The teacher should find a happy compromise between allowing the child to follow their first instincts and waiting for a moment or two to extend their communicative abilities.

The teacher may also like to try a number of variations on this theme including a metallic or brightly coloured wig, funny spectacles, goggly eyes, lipstick spots/freckles, false moustache or beard.

Using a final twist to this theme, the teacher can wear a series of rubber masks that are available from seaside arcades or joke shops. These allow the teacher to take on a range of characteristics for a few moments and add to the event.

Evaluative Criteria   The children should make eye contact and use some interactive and communicative behaviours.

Causal significance   *In what way did the teacher look different; can you look different as well?*

Tiger, Tiger

(with apologies to W. Blake)

Social Play	Three
Play Stage	Func/Sym
Group	Individual or Group
Affect	High

Activity

The teacher crouches on the floor and looking intently at the child chants 'Tiger, Tiger, burning bright, catching (child's name) in the night'.

On saying the child's name, the teacher makes a tickling or pouncing gesture towards the child. The teacher should use animated gesture, action and facial expression to state the fierce aspects of the tiger's character.

Evaluative Criteria   The child makes eye contact and moves towards the teacher, or makes a tickle gesture or attempts to repeat the rhyme or the word 'Tiger'.

Causal significance   *Prediction . . . do you know when the tiger will pounce? Did you read the signs?*

Furniture Removals		
	Social Play	Six
	Play Stage	Rel/Func /Sym
	Group	Usually 2 or 3 children
	Affect	Low
Activity	The children are asked to move a large (but not too heavy) item of furniture. This might be a very large piece of wood, a huge cardboard box or a light table. The children must work together to negotiate the large object through doorways and around difficult obstacles. Dissenters should be encouraged to re-join the group in their efforts.	
Evaluative Criteria	The children must try to share the task and work collaboratively. This activity immediately demonstrates if one child is not helping and their task is visually obvious. The children might use some forms of communication to help in their task.	
Causal significance	*We are all working together to achieve a common aim. Why did the table not go through the door? Who should have helped to get it through? Could the other child see that you needed help? Did you tell him that you needed help?*	

Blindfold		
	Social Play	Five
	Play Stage	Func/Sym
	Group	Group
	Affect	Moderate to High
Activity	The children are arranged in a semi-circle and each child holds an object. The teacher wears a blindfold and has to walk amongst the group and identify what each child is holding.	
	The teacher may also try some other activities such as blindfold juggling, blindfold building towers with blocks or blindfold dressing up. Care should be taken in all blindfold activities.	
Evaluative Criteria	The children should be interested in or enjoy the process and wish to engage with the games.	
Causal significance	*The blindfolded child's perception of the objects may or may not be correct. The belief based on this perception may or may not be incorrect.*	

Poorly Teacher

Social Play
Play Stage — Seven
Group — Rel/Func /Sym
Affect — Individual or Group — Moderate or Low

Activity

The teacher feigns serious injury on entering the room. The children are required to help the teacher with immediate medical intervention. A bag full of bandages, needle-less syringes, stethoscopes, eye-patches, empty plastic bottles of medicine and tablets, teaspoons, slings and splints are emptied onto the floor. The children are able to administer a range of treatments to the ailing teacher.

Evaluative Criteria

The children should engage with the activity and respond to specific requests for attention. For example, 'Oww ... my foot hurts ... Oh dear ... I'm feeling dizzy'. Some children may ask if the teacher is feeling better.

Causal significance

Did the teacher need help? Why? What sort of help did you give? What sort of help was needed? Was s/he happy when hurt? Was s/he happy after you helped? Were you asked for help or did you know that it was needed?

Where's the Bag?

Social Play
Play Stage — Eight
Group — Higher Sym
Affect — Individual or Group — Moderate or High

Activity

The teacher walks into the room and leaves a bag or another important object in an easily visible place near the group. The teacher remembers that he or she has left something elsewhere and tells the children that s/he will return in a few moments.

Another (subversive) teacher in the group tells the children that they should play a trick: they should hide the teacher's bag. When the teacher returns, the bag has disappeared.

The teacher looks hard and long at the place where the bag was last seen and says in an exaggerated voice, 'I can't believe my eyes ... my bag has disappeared'. The teacher leaves the room, clutching head and looking confused.

The subversive asks the children 'Where did the teacher (name) look for the bag?' If the children can answer this correctly, the subversive asks 'Where did the teacher (name) think the bag would be?' and finally asks 'Where is the bag really?'

The subversive agrees with the children to return the bag to the original position. On returning, the teacher is greeted with the bag and shows suitably incredulous surprise and joy.

Evaluative Criteria

The children should be able to remember and describe where the teacher left the bag. Some may remember her expression of shock at the missing bag and answer the question about the teacher's memory of the bag's location. All the children should be able to say where the bag was really hidden.

Causal significance

The first teacher does not realise that the bag is missing: where does s/he expect it to be? Where is it really? Could the teacher know where it is hidden if s/he did not see us? Did the teacher want the bag – how did s/he feel when it was missing?

Appendix C: Guidelines for drama with children with autism

A common difficulty when teaching drama with children with autism is that decisions often have to be made at considerable speed, in order to sustain the momentum of the drama and keep everyone focused. At times, their suggestions may be unforthcoming or else so limited that the teacher feels obliged to follow a particular line of development, however unpromising in terms of learning potential. At other times, the teacher may face a choice between several responses at once, and want to give gratification to all of them, at the risk of becoming distracted away from 'the plot'. Neither of these extreme tacks is desirable: the teacher needs to find ways to compromise and inject other possibilities (which the children should have the right to reject) and at times be prepared to make executive decisions.

At times too, the responses of children with autism can seem quite bizarre, and yet gentle probing may reveal a logic intrinsic to that particular child. Teachers need to acquire the skill of converting the child's *intention* almost instantaneously, to make it compatible with the evolving shared fiction. Morgan and Saxton (1987) identify certain techniques for competent drama teachers to acquire:

- *slowing down* – to focus the children on a significant moment rather than rush on;
- *filling in* – contributing information as background and a basis for negotiation;
- *building volume* – deepening participants' commitment and emotional involvement;
- *crystallising* – employing a particular strategy or drama convention in order to focus on a meaningful moment and prompt reflection;
- *unifying* – bringing disparate threads together to achieve a group consensus.

A competent drama teacher will be able to recognise certain factors within any situation and respond accordingly:

- understanding the drama process (see Chapter 5);
- identifying a potential learning area and organising the drama into a 'meaning frame' or 'focusing lens' (Neelands 1984);
- accommodating contextual factors (strengths and interests of staff and children, space and time available, institutional constraints such as noise thresholds and staffing ratio);
- making appropriate decisions based on possible strategies (see below).

Initially it may be helpful for teachers new to drama to go through a mental checklist, based on the pointers below. In time however, the experienced teacher may come to make such decisions more intuitively on the spot, and synthesise all the variables in the teaching situation automatically. The following suggestions (formulated originally through research at the University of Cambridge Institute of Education) offer a repertoire of possibilities for the drama teacher working with children with autism.

Establish a clear context for the make-believe

- Explain to the children what is happening – talk them into the drama; for example, 'in a moment [when I put this hat on] I'll be pretending to be somebody else'.
- Ensure the children's attention is fully gained before starting the drama, and that they have a clear focus; for example, ensure you establish where the drama will be taking place, what they will be doing and who they will be pretending to be.
- Be prepared to stop the drama quickly to cross-check out of role that everyone is 'with it'; use a clear visual signal to indicate when talking in and out of role (for example, a hat that is easily removed and replaced).
- Build belief in the drama initially through discussion with the teacher-in-role, rather than having the children 'disperse' and risk losing focus; it is important for the children to think about who they are in the drama and what they are doing, to be made explicitly aware of their thoughts and feelings and attitudes.
- Involve the children in adapting the space for the drama, to help them into the symbolism, and to allow time for them to 'catch on' to what is happening.
- Encourage cross-fertilisation of ideas through strategies that mix the children up; for example, groupings of children, supported by strategically placed staff.
- Be prepared to move the drama on (for example using a narrative link) to allow sufficient time to de-role, in order to reflect and discuss the drama afterwards – this is crucial for children with autism, to transfer learning from the make-believe to the real world.
- Allow sufficient time for drama when timetabling – do not underestimate 'time for talk' afterwards, and gauge how long children may be able to sustain

concentration – check the extent to which timetabling may allow the possibility to plan for drama more flexibly.

- Move the narrative forwards or backwards to examine particular moments of significance in the drama; for example, strategies such as 'action replay', 'freeze frame' and 'fast-forwarding' and 're-winding'.
- Be prepared to stop the drama and carry it over to the following session to get the most out of each situation, rather than rush it through; use of video can help children with autism to 'sustain the plot', as well as be a useful means to teach them the nature of narrative.
- Consider completing an unfinished drama through cross-curricular work related to the drama, so that the pupils still feel they are 'doing drama'.
- Communicate signals and intentions clearly and unambiguously, and 'prop the role' to distinguish between the make-believe and the real world.

Engage children with autism on a feeling level

- Make the drama relevant to the group, so that the children can 'hook' into it – relating to feeling thirsty in a hot country or desert may be beyond their actual experience of the world.
- Work from the concrete: provide children with autism with a genuine 'felt' experience in the drama, from which then to abstract; for example, being deliberately affronted by the official in the Monet's garden drama, and having their reaction subsequently described as angry.
- Teach that actions have consequences, if necessary by including opportunities to repeat experiences; for example, teacher-in-role could find a succession of excuses to leave a situation, to give the children a chance to draw on their resources.
- Enable the children to see the consequences of their actions and decisions: go with their responses but be on the look-out to explore their implications, retaining the notion of challenging their play.
- Find ways to discuss, question and reflect on events, both in the drama and out of role, cross-checking to ensure everyone is 'with it'; for example, using 'thinks bubbles' to access a particular character's thoughts, watching a piece of 'theatre', freezing the action and questioning the children about a significant moment.
- Develop the drama in small increments, through strategies of rehearsal and repetition, such as action replay, so that the children are able to grasp the significance of an incident.
- Provide a clear focus and sense of purpose; for example, questioning the children ahead of an improvisation, about what they will be doing.
- Use 'negative role' to enable the children to contribute to the drama: they may not be able to suggest what to do, but the incongruity of the inappropriate may prompt them into a response, even correcting the inept teacher-in-role.

- Develop questioning skills to empower the children, varying between open and closed questions to enable them to respond and make decisions or choices.
- Be prepared to state boundaries, as paradoxically this may enable a child with autism to make a creative contribution – a clear choice within constraints.

Employ strategies to 'contain' children with autism

- Use inherently directive strategies to organise the children in the drama space; for example, allocating groupings of children to particular areas.
- Be sensitive to the social demands from particular strategies; for example, certain children with autism will find it very difficult to wait until everyone is organised before starting the drama.
- Use visually interesting props to help rivet the children's attention; for example, a cardboard box covered in spangly paper.
- Deal with management issues as far as possible in role; for example, an authority figure may legitimately ask for silence before proceeding.
- Teaching in role will help focus the children's attention and give the feeling that the drama is under way, particularly if it is used to 'set frame' – for example, 'Good morning, my team of gardeners.'
- Have the children instruct an inept teacher-in-role – children with autism may find this role-reversal, where they have become experts, intriguing and motivating.
- Anticipate certain volatile moments and be ready with a containing kind of strategy; for example, a meeting, a ritual, use of strategically placed supporting staff among the children.
- Develop a repertoire of containing strategies that could involve the whole group, yet with elements of freedom in them; for example, a contextualised drama game, a Prescribed Drama Structure, a song, a ritual.
- Use strategies with a strong visual element to focus attention and bring the group together; for example, forum theatre (questioning a teacher-in-role).

Accommodate purposefully a range of abilities in children with autism

- Link a more able peer with a child with autism in improvisations as an appropriate role model and support.
- Use a more able peer to model an appropriate response for his/her peers with autism.
- Use closed questions (yes/no) to empower non-verbal or reticent children with autism; their status can still be elevated, if this involves making a key decision.
- Use multi-sensory materials to support the spoken word, to access meaning to children with autism; for example, sound tapes, pictures, textiles, real objects.

- Keep a stock of basic props, hats, pictures, and lengths of material that can be used flexibly and called upon instantly as visual hooks to clarify meaning should the need arise.
- Incorporate strategies that can embrace children with autism purposefully at all levels of ability; for example a Prescribed Drama Structure.
- Use levelling strategies, such as everyone finding one word to describe a situation.
- Challenge higher attaining children to demonstrate leadership qualities, and to cooperate and negotiate in collaborative work.
- Challenge lower attaining children through judicious groupings, and allocate a supporting member of staff sensitively to elicit responses.
- Aim to reach all of the children some of the time.
- Ensure that everyone is given a role, no matter how vestigial – drama is a group experience, and it is important that it is perceived as such.

Use strategies to keep children with autism 'on task'

- Break up the drama into a series of activities (mixture of discussion, static and active physical tasks) to create an ebb and flow, enabling children with a short concentration span to come and go and focus attention better.
- Develop a repertoire of drama conventions – maximise options for organising the drama according to the children's mood.
- Consciously develop the children's knowledge of different strategies to enable them to negotiate the way the drama is to be organised – they will be more likely to focus attention on something in which they have made an investment.
- Make the children's suggestions and initiatives coherent as far as possible, so that they fit the context of the drama, relating them if necessary to the intention behind the contribution, and rephrasing and/or elaborating on them – this will help the children see their responses harnessed, and to feel 'ownership' of the material.
- Slow the drama down through the use of thoughtful, reflective 'static' strategies; for example, moments of 'theatre' or a ritual, and discussion both in and out of role to elicit their responses.
- Question the children to keep them focused and on task; for example, 'is this a difficult floor to mop? Show me how hard you have to use the mop!'
- Use a member of staff in an indeterminate role to help mix up peer groups and challenge the children and help keep them focused during improvisations.
- Limit the amount of listening required, as children with autism may lose concentration if they cannot take in a verbal flow; for example, make succinct narrative links, or deliberately stumble over words in a narrative, so that the children fill in the missing words to tell the story.
- Work immediately in role to avoid complex language structures, and to bring

meaning into the here-and-now; this will enable children with autism to respond spontaneously, rather than to try to predict 'what would you do if . . . '.

- Pace the drama – faster, punchier delivery to maintain their attention; avoid getting 'bogged down' in seeing through a plan.
- Look out for opportunities to introduce tension, to help sustain motivation and attention; for example, changes in moments of high excitement (teacher-in-role with urgent announcement) contrasted with a moment of stillness and quiet reflection.
- Consider stopping the drama at a high point of tension, to motivate the children to want to know more, but use this very selectively, as children with autism may not be able to cope with a seemingly unresolved situation.
- Use closed questions selectively (used inappropriately they can be unnecessarily limiting) to create a sense of urgency and to consolidate the action.
- Model an appropriate response through use of role, particularly using supporting staff strategically to generate atmosphere.
- Ensure that required props are to hand and that any tapes are in the right place, to avoid breaking the tension of the fiction and the children's fragile concentration – momentum is easily lost by small details such as these if the drama is interrupted.
- Minimise distractions, 'traffic' through the drama space and other disruptions by negotiating ahead for use of available space.

Work to the strengths and interests of both children with autism and supporting staff

- Develop proficiency in different kinds of role (authoritative, someone in need of help, someone carrying out orders who may become a potential ally – someone to whom the group have to explain themselves) (see Chapter 6).
- Be aware of the preferences of certain children with autism for particular kinds of role; for example, if a child is intimidated by a high status teacher-in-role.
- Be prepared to compromise an individual's idea for the sake of the majority group feeling – this can be a hard (but important) learning point for certain children! Be sure to reject the idea, not the child, however: 'log' the idea, as something to come back to another time.
- Be prepared to follow the children's ideas and suggestions and trust to their initiative, and be on the look out for a learning area to arise in process – occasionally it can be difficult to deflect the wishes of a child with autism!
- Be prepared to block (sensitively) an initiative by a child with autism, if this is inappropriate to the context: encourage them to see why their idea may not be viable.
- Be aware of individual needs, and find ways to access the material so that it is perceived as relevant and meaningful by the child.

- Be sensitive to group dynamics involving children with autism, and aim to maximise tolerance levels and acceptance of social space being shared, to develop positive relationships.
- While obsessive interests can be a useful starting point for drama work, consider also the age-appropriateness of the material, and whether a balance needs to be reached.
- Find roles appropriate to the children, according to the kind of challenge they may need, and ensuring that everyone has a part, however vague or ill-defined at first.
- Ensure that all the children are enabled to contribute ideas for the drama, however small – they will be more likely to concentrate, if they perceive the drama as theirs.
- Differentiate drama planning to cater for the range of ability within the group – some drama conventions and strategies are more challenging (see Chapters 5 and 6), while others can reach children of different abilities at the same time (for example, a Prescribed Drama Structure, a ritual, a song).
- Use a confident colleague (teacher or teaching assistant) in a 'character' role if they are willing and capable of holding the drama together – this can build in a few moments of precious 'thinking time' for the teacher, and enable him or her to observe from the edge.
- With more anxious staff ('Oh no, I haven't got to act, have I?'), or where staff are fairly new to working together, find a role for them that is on the edge of the action but which can be developed flexibly to allow them to be more central, or to take a legitimate view from the side.
- Use supporting staff strategically to deal with an individual child or isolated management matter, rather than risk losing the group through the teacher diverting his or her attention.
- If the drama feels as if it is not working, it may be possible to stop and turn the onus back on the children: 'This isn't working! What would make our drama more exciting?' At worst, it is always possible to stop altogether, rather than struggle on against the odds.
- Brief assistant staff ahead of the lesson, so that they have a clear idea of what is expected and their part in the proceedings; this will help staff becoming carried away and hi-jacking the drama inadvertently in their enthusiasm!
- Develop a discreet signalling system with supporting staff to use within the drama.
- Check other commitments supporting staff may have (for example lunchtime duties, bus escort), and plan the drama accordingly around their availability, and to minimise interruptions to the drama.
- Build in time to gain feedback from staff supporting the session – they may well have noticed a child's response that the teacher caught up in the thick of the action may have missed – they may have been briefed to track (discreetly) certain children.

Appendix D: Resources for teaching play and drama

In the development of early play, children with autism need a wide range of attractive objects that can be used to extend their interest and their use of these materials within social contexts. These need to be aligned to their developmental needs: some children will require materials that have interesting and contrasting sensory qualities; others will require objects that can be ordered, arranged, inserted, or built upon. Similarly, it is necessary to have a range of attractive objects for children with autism who are able to play at higher levels. It is essential that a range of items and equipment is available, that are good quality and robust, attractive, in good repair – and safe. These materials are a key resource and require careful planning and financing as an educational priority.

Children who are capable of pretence require some play materials that are representational and some that are not. Representational objects look like what they are supposed to be: a toy car looks like a real car and a rubber snake looks like a real snake. They also require non-representational objects that do not particularly resemble anything else and which can be used flexibly; for example, lengths of fabric, cardboard boxes and plasticine. Similarly, a collection of props for drama requires some clearly representational items (for example: bags, hats, an apron, official peaked cap), but also flexible items such as long lengths of fabric (for costume or as scenery), masking tape (for delineating areas in the drama space), paper and pens. It is helpful too, to build up a collection of pictorial images to help support the spoken word, and enable children with autism to participate meaningfully.

The tendency of some children with autism to eat inappropriate objects can force restrictions on the provision of certain materials in some instances. Particular care should be taken to supervise use of materials that could be harmful if swallowed. For some children, this could include materials such as playdough, which contain gluten to which they may have intolerance. Paint and glues can also be attractive to some children. Care is required also if materials can be broken down into small pieces and swallowed. Objects can sometimes constitute an unanticipated hazard when used inappropriately or unwittingly: for example, a toy hammer for a pegboard may assume disproportional danger in the hands of certain children.

While it is important that teachers of children with autism should discuss with parents how their child's needs can be met at home and school, it is critical that everyone is aware of issues regarding eating, drinking or smelling of inappropriate objects. It is also important that the teacher involved in play uses a sound understanding of each child in considering how each of the materials might be used or misused. Individual sensory sensitivities and intolerances can also be highly idiosyncratic – certain sound frequencies, for example.

A list of materials suitable for teaching play to children with autism covering a range of abilities might include the following:

Long lengths of material: coloured, textured, lustrous or furry fabrics. These can be turned into anything (well almost anything). Bed sheets or a parachute can be made into houses, caves, jellyfish and oceans.

Cardboard boxes of different sizes: a wonderful resource which with a little imagination can be turned into cars, boats and aeroplanes, buildings, furniture or food, hats, masks or animal costumes.

Clean plastic bottles: to be used as rockets and aeroplanes, bombs and missiles, fish, sharks and dolphins, containers of magic powder, the school bell, or given a face, can be transformed into little people.

Bags of different sizes and descriptions: these can be turned into houses, mouths, bats, birds, hats . . . or just be bags.

Percussion instruments: for creating sounds in different ways (shaking, tapping, blowing, scraping); producing different dynamics (loud, quiet); varying sound qualities (wooden and metal instruments, with a selection of beaters of varying hardness); exploring high and low sounds; making long and short sounds (ringing, echoing, reverberating, clipped). For example: maracas, hand drum (tambour), tambourine, large crash cymbal, claves (or short lengths of wooden dowel), duck call, cuckoo call, swanee whistle, guiro, individual chime bars, wooden xylophone, metallophone, keyboard.

Moulding materials: plasticine, playdough (gluten-free), clay, cornflour.

Found sources: sticky tape, cotton wool, string, thick coloured rope, wire pipe-cleaners, newspaper, cellophane, egg-boxes, wooden sticks, wheels, water, tubes, feathers, ribbons, hoops and bangles, samples of fabric and glittery materials.

Props for make-believe: soft toys, puppets, dolls, masks, plastic people and animals, toy cars and other vehicles, kitchen and dining room equipment, items for getting washed and dressed, dressing-up costumes, train sets, dolls houses, garage, coins, plastic food, suitcase/rucksack, shoes, boots, sub-aqua fins, crown, tiara, fairy-wand (toy guns and swords), cash till, fantasy TV characters.

Role-play area: a large themed play house/shop/factory/garage/repair and maintenance shop/hospital/dentist/optician's/fire or police station/café/restaurant/ post office/airport departure lounge/hairdresser's or fairy-tale castle.

Sensory objects: shiny plastic boxes, transparent bottles containing beads, spinning or revolving objects, stacking beakers, ring tower, shape posting box, eye-catching bead necklace, springy telephone cables, pendulums, windmills, large marbles and balls, things in boxes, bags or pockets, percussion instruments, soft and hard hairbrushes, things connected with elastic, rain-stick, things that balance, marble-run, things that are stuck with Velcro, squashy cushions, balloons, a bunch of keys and key rings, ribbons and ropes with objects sewn on, things that vibrate, things that are cold/warm, polystyrene squiggles, wooden sticks, purses, screw-top plastic jars or cardboard boxes each containing a different toy, scratch and sniff patches, stickers and stamps, things to lie on that are furry, plastic, crinkly or soft, things to hide inside or things to bounce on.

References

Aherne, P. *et al.* (1990) *Communication for All.* London: David Fulton Publishers.

Aylott, J. and Rickard, G. (2001) 'Art and autism: facilitating the environment for creative expression', *Good Autism Practice*, March, 67–75.

Baldwin, P. (1998) 'Drama and literacy', *Drama*, **5** (3), 15–18.

Baron-Cohen, S. (1988) 'Social and pragmatic deficits in autism: psychological or affective?', *Journal of Autism and Developmental Disorders*, **18**, 379–402.

Baron-Cohen, S. (1989) 'The theory of mind hypothesis of autism: a reply to Boucher', *British Journal of Disorders of Communication*, **24**, 199–200.

Baron-Cohen, S. (ed.) (1993) *Understanding Other Minds: perspectives from autism.* Oxford: Oxford University Press.

Bates, E. *et al.* (1979) *The Emergence of Symbols: cognition and communication in infancy.* New York: Academic Press.

Beyer, J. and Gammeltoft, L. (2000) *Autism and Play.* London: Jessica Kingsley.

Boal, A. (1981) *Theatre de l'opprime*, Numero 5. Ceditade: An 03.

Bolton, G. (1979) *Towards a Theory of Drama in Education.* Harlow: Longman.

Bolton, G. (1986) *Selected Writings on Drama and Education.* London and New York: Longman.

Bolton, G. (1992) *New Perspectives on Classroom Drama.* London: Simon and Schuster.

Booth, D. (1994) *Story Drama.* Pembroke Publishers.

Brown, E. (1996) *Religious Education for All.* London: David Fulton Publishers.

Bruce, T. (1991) *Time to Play in Early Childhood Education.* London: Hodder and Stoughton.

Bruner, J. (1975a) 'The ontogenesis of speech acts'. *Journal of Child Language*, **2**, 1–19.

Bruner, J. (1975b) 'From communication to language: a psychological perspective', *Cognition*, **3**, 255–87.

Bruner, J. (1986) *Actual Minds, Possible Worlds.* Cambridge, MA: Harvard University Press.

Bruner, J. and Feldman, C. (1993) 'Theories of mind and the problem of autism', in Baron-Cohen, S. *et al.* (eds) *Understanding Other Minds: perspectives from autism.* Oxford: Oxford University Press.

Bryant, P.E. and Bradley, L. (1985) *Children's Reading Problems.* Oxford: Blackwell.

Cecil, L.M. *et al.* (1985) 'Curiosity-exploration-play: the early childhood mosaic'. *Early Child Development and Care*, **19**, 199–217.

Charman, T. and Baron-Cohen, S. (1997) 'Brief report: prompted pretend play in autism', *Journal of Autism and Developmental Disorders*, **27** (3), 325–32.

Chesner, A. (1995) *Dramatherapy for People with Learning Disabilities.* London: Jessica Kingsley.

Chukovsky, K. (1963) *From Two to Five.* Berkeley, CA: University of California Press.

Cicchetti, D. *et al.* (1994) 'Symbolic development in children with Down Syndrome and in children with autism: an organisational, developmental psychopathological perspective', in Slade, A. and Palmer Wolf, D. (eds) *Children at Play: clinical approaches to meaning and representation.* New York: Oxford University Press.

Clethero, S. (2001) 'An exploration into creativity', *Good Autism Practice*, March, 45–51.

Collis, M. and Lacey, P. (1996) *Interactive Approaches to Teaching and Learning.* London: David Fulton Publishers.

Corsaro, W. (1986) 'Discourse processes within peer culture: from a constructivist to an interpretative approach to childhood socialisation', *Sociological Studies of Child Development*, 1, 81–101.

Crozier, W.R. (1997) *Individual Learners: personality differences in education.* London: Routledge.

Cumine, V. *et al.* (2000) *Autism in the Early Years.* London: David Fulton Publishers.

Damasio, A. (1999) *The Feeling of What Happens.* London: William Heinemann.

Damasio, A.R. and Maurer, R.G. (1978) 'A neurological model for autism', *Archives of Neurology*, 35, 777–86.

Deci, E.L. and Ryan, R.M. (1985) *Intrinsic Motivation and Self Determination in Human Behaviour.* New York: Plenum.

DES/WO (1990) *English in the National Curriculum, No. 2* (Statutory Order for English). London: HMSO.

DfEE (1998) *The National Literacy Strategy.* London: DfEE.

DfEE (1999) *All Our Futures: creativity, culture and education* (Report by the National Advisory Committee on Creative and Cultural Education). Sudbury: DfEE.

DfES (2001a) *The National Literacy Strategy – Teaching writing: support material for text level objectives. Flier 2: Writing narrative.* London: DfES.

DfES (2001b) *The National Literacy Strategy – Teaching writing: support material for text level objectives. Flier 4: Writing playscripts.* London: DfES.

Duffy, B. (1998) *Supporting Creativity and Imagination in the Early Years.* Buckingham: Open University Press.

Edwards, S. (1999) *Speaking and Listening for All.* London: David Fulton Publishers.

Eyre, D. (1997) *Able Children in Ordinary Schools.* London: David Fulton Publishers.

Faulkner, D. (1995) 'Play, self and the social world', in Barnes, P. (ed.) *Personal, Social and Emotional Development of Children.* Oxford: Blackwell/The Open University.

Fein, G.G. (1984) 'The self-building potential of pretend play or "I got a fish, all by myself" ', in Yawkey, T.D. and Pellegrini, A.D. (eds) *Child's Play: developmental and applied.* Hillsdale, NJ: Lawrence Erlbaum Associates.

Frith, U. (1989) *Autism: explaining the enigma.* London: Blackwell.

Gallagher, J.J. (1985) *Teaching the Gifted Child.* Newton: Allyn and Bacon.

George, D. (1992) *The Challenge of the Able Child.* London: David Fulton Publishers.

Gilham, G. (1974) 'Condercum School Report'. Unpublished paper, Newcastle-upon-Tyne LEA.

Goldbart, J. (1988) 'Communication for a purpose', in Coupe, J. and Goldbart, J. (eds) *Communication Before Speech.* London: Croom Helm.

Grandin, T. (1997) 'Mind-readers' (producer/director Taylor, J.). All Illuminations Production for Channel 4.

Gregory, R.L. (1977) 'Psychology: towards a science of fiction', in Meek, M. *et al.* (eds) *The Cool Web. The Pattern of Children's Reading.* London: Bodley Head.

Grove, N. and Park, K. (2001) *Social Cognition through Drama and Literature for People with Learning Disabilities.* London: Jessica Kingsley.

Gulbenkian Report (1982) *The Arts in Schools.* London: Calouste Gulbenkian Foundation.

Harris, J. (1994) 'Language, communication and personal power: a developmental perspective', in Coupe O'Kane, J. and Smith, B. (eds) *Taking Control.* London: David Fulton Publishers.

Harris, P.L. (2000) *The Work of the Imagination.* Oxford: Blackwell.

Harris, P.L. and Levers, H.J. (2000) 'Pretending, imagery and self-awareness in autism', in *Understanding Other Minds*, volume 2. Oxford: Oxford University Press.

Hobson, J.A. and Stickgold, R. (1994) 'A neurocognitive approach to dreaming', *Consciousness and Cognition*, **3** (1), 1–15.

Howes, C. (1992) *The Collaborative Construction of Pretend: social pretend play functions.* Albany: State University of New York Press.

Hutt, C. (1979) 'Play in the under fives: form, development and function', in Howells, J.G. (ed.) *Modern Perspectives in the Psychiatry of Infancy*. New York: Bruner Marcel.

Iveson, S.D. (1996) 'Communication in the mind'. Paper to the International Congress of Psychology XXVI Montreal. *International Journal of Psychology*, **31**, 254.

Jarrold, C. *et al.* (1993) 'Symbolic play in autism: a review', *Journal of Autism and Developmental Disorders*, **23** (2), 281–8.

Jarrold, C. *et al.* (1996) 'Generative deficits in pretend play in autism', *British Journal of Developmental Psychology*, **14**, 275–300.

Jones, R. (1996) *Emerging Patterns of Literacy. a multi-disciplinary perspective.* London: Routledge.

Jordan, R. (1999) *Autistic Spectrum Disorders.* London: David Fulton Publishers.

Jordan, R. and Powell, S. (1995) *Understanding and Teaching Children with Autism.* Chichester: Wiley and Sons.

Jordan, R. *et al.* (2001) 'Unit 7: access to the academic curriculum', *Curriculum and Approaches for Children with Autism* (module code 11 05505/11470). Birmingham: The University of Birmingham, Faculty of Education and Continuing Studies, School of Education.

Kaufman, B.N. (1976) *To Love is to be Happy with.* London: Souvenir Press.

Kaufman, B.N. (1994) *Son Rise: the miracle continues.* Tiburon, CA: H.J. Kramer Inc.

Kitson, N. (1994) '"Please Miss Alexander: will you be the robber?" Fantasy play: a case for adult intervention', in Moyles, J. (ed.) *The Excellence of Play.* Buckingham: Open University Press.

Klin, A. (1991) 'Young autistic children's listening preferences in regard to speech: a possible characterization of the symptom of social withdrawal', *Journal of Autism and Developmental Disorders*, **23** (10), 15–35.

Klin, A. *et al.* (1992) 'Autistic social dysfunction: some limitations of theory of mind hypothesis', *Journal of Child Psychology and Psychiatry*, **33**, 861–76.

Leekam, S.R. *et al.* (1997) 'Eye-direction detection: a dissociation between geometric and joint attention skills in autism', *British Journal of Developmental Psychology*, **17**, 77–95.

Leslie, A.M. (1987) 'Pretence and representation: the origins of theory of mind', *Psychological Review*, **94**, 412–26.

Leslie, A. (1994) 'Pretending and believing: issues in the theory of ToMM', *Cognition*, **50**, 211–38.

Lewis, V. and Boucher, J. (1998) *The Test of Pretend Play.* London: The Psychological Corporation.

Libby, S. *et al.* (1998) 'Spontaneous play in children with autism: a reappraisal', *Journal of Autism and Developmental Disorders*, **28** (6), 487–97.

Lillard, A. (1994) 'Making sense of pretence', in Lewis, C. and Mitchell, P. (eds) *Children's Early Understanding of Mind.* Hove: Erlbaum.

Lowe, M. and Costello, A.J. (1989) *Symbolic Play Test.* Windsor: NFER-Nelson.

McKellar, P. (1957) *Imagination and Thinking: a psychological analysis.* London: Cohen and West.

McLean, J. and Snyder-McLean, L. (1985) *Developmentally early communicative behaviours among severely retarded adolescents (Seminal Topic Outline).* Hester Adrian Centre: University of Manchester.

Mitchell, S. (1994) 'Some Implications of the High/Scope Curriculum and the Education of Children with Learning Difficulties', in Coupe O'Kane, J. and Smith, B. (eds) *Taking Control: enabling people with learning difficulties.* London: David Fulton Publishers.

Monks, F.J. (1992) 'Development of gifted children: the issue of identification and programming', in Monks, F.J. and Peters, W. (eds) *Talent for the Future.* Assen/Maastricht: Van Gorcum.

Morgan, N. and Saxton, J. (1987) *Teaching Drama.* London: Hutchinson.

Moyles, J. (1989) *Just Playing?* Milton Keynes: Open University Press.

Mundy, P. (1995) 'Joint attention and social-emotional approach behavior in children with autism', *Development and Psychopathology*, 7, 63–82.

Mundy, P. and Crowson, M. (1997) 'Joint attention and early social communication: implications for research on intervention with autism', *Journal of Autism and Developmental Disorders*, 27 (6), 653–7.

Neelands, J. (1984) *Making Sense of Drama*. London: Heinemann.

Neelands, J. (2000) 'Foreword – Live Language', in Ackroyd, J. (ed.) *Literacy Alive! Drama projects for literacy learning*. London: Hodder and Stoughton.

Nelson, K. (1986) *Event Knowledge: structure and function in development*. Hillsdale (N.J.): Lawrence Erlbaum Associates.

Newson, E. (2000) 'Using humour to enable flexibility and social empathy in children with Asperger's Syndrome: some practical strategies', in Powell, S. (ed.) *Helping Children with Autism to Learn*. London: David Fulton Publishers.

Nind, M. and Hewett, D. (1994, reprinted 1995) *Access to Communication*. London: David Fulton Publishers.

Peeters, T. (2000) 'The language of objects', in Powell, S. (ed.) *Helping Children with Autism to Learn*. London: David Fulton Publishers.

Peter, M. (1994) *Drama for All*. London: David Fulton Publishers.

Peter, M. (1995) *Making Drama Special*. London: David Fulton Publishers.

Peter, M. (1996a) *Art For All, vol. 1 (the Framework) and vol. 2 (the Practice)*. London: David Fulton Publishers.

Peter, M. (1996b) 'Developing drama from story', in Kempe, A. (ed.) *Drama Education and Special Needs*. Cheltenham: Stanley Thornes.

Peter, M. (1997) 'The Arts for All?', *PMLD Link*, 27 (Spring), 2–5.

Peter, M. (1998) 'Good for them, or what? The arts and pupils with SEN', *British Journal of Special Education*, 25 (4), 168–72.

Peter, M. (2000a) 'Drama: communicating with people with learning disabilities', *Nursing and Residential Care*, 2 (2), February, 78–82.

Peter, M. (2000b) 'Developing Drama with Children with Autism', *Good Autism Practice*, 1 (1), May, 9–20.

Potter, C. and Whittaker, C. (2001) *Enabling Communication in Children with Autism*. London: Jessica Kingsley.

Powell, S. and Jordan, R. (1997) *Autism and Learning*. London: David Fulton Publishers.

Prevezer, W. (2000) 'Musical Interaction and Children with Autism', in Powell, S. (ed.) *Helping Children with Autism to Learn*. London: David Fulton Publishers.

Prokofiev, F. (1994) 'The role of an Art Therapist, part 4: Different Roles', *Art, Craft, Design and Technology*, October, 22–3.

Purdie, H. (1996) 'Music is a world', *In Touch*, Summer, 33.

QCA (1999) *The National Curriculum*. London: HMSO.

QCA (2000) *Curriculum Guidance for the Foundation Stage*. Sudbury: QCA.

QCA (2001a) *Planning, teaching and assessing the curriculum for pupils with learning difficulties: Developing skills*. Sudbury: QCA.

QCA (2001b) *Planning, teaching and assessing the curriculum for pupils with learning difficulties: English*. Sudbury: QCA.

QCA (2001c) *Planning, teaching and assessing the curriculum for pupils with learning difficulties: Personal, Social and Health Education and Citizenship*. Sudbury: QCA.

Reynell, J.K. (1977) *Reynell Developmental Language Scales: a second revision*. NFER-Nelson.

Sachs, J. *et al.* (1985) 'Narratives in preschoolers' sociodramatic play: the role of knowledge and communicative competence', in Galda, L. and Pellegrini, A.D. (eds) *Play, Language and Stories: the development of children's literate behaviour*. Norwood, NJ: Abblex Publishing Corporation.

Schneider, E. (1999) *Discovering My Autism*. London: Jessica Kingsley.

Schopler, E. and Olley, J. G. (1982) 'Comprehensive educational services for autistic children: the TEACCH model', in Reynolds, C.R. and Gutkin, T.R. (eds) *Handbook of School Psychology*. New York: Wiley.

Sheppard, D. (1991) 'Developing drama and art in primary schools', in Sullivan, M. (ed.) *Supporting Change and Development in the Primary School*. Harlow. Longman.

Sheppard, D. (1994) 'Other People's Stories'. Keynote address to the National Drama conference (unpublished paper), Manchester Metropolitan University.

Sherborne, V. (1990) *Developmental Movement for Children*. Cambridge: Cambridge University Press.

Sherratt, D. (1999) 'The importance of play', *Good Autism Practice*, September, 23–31.

Sherratt, D. (2001) 'Play, Performance, Symbols and Affect', in Richer, J. and Coates, S. (eds) *Autism: the Search for Coherence*. London: Jessica Kingsley.

Sherratt, D. (2002) 'Developing pretend play in children with autism: an intervention study', *Autism: The International Journal of Research and Practice*, **6** (2).

Singer, D. and Singer, J. (1990) *The House of Make-believe: children's play and the developing imagination*. Cambridge, Mass.: Harvard University Press.

Stahmer, A. and Stahmer, A.C. (1995) 'Teaching symbolic play skills to children with autism using pivotal response training', *Journal of Autism and Developmental Disorders*, **25**, 123–41.

Stern, D. (1985) *The Interpersonal World of the Infant*. New York: Basic Books.

Tager-Flusberg, H. (1993) 'What language reveals about the understanding of mind in children with autism', in Baron-Cohen, S. *et al.* (eds) *Understanding Other Minds: Perspectives from Autism*. Oxford: Oxford University Press.

Taylor, J. (1984) 'Steps to Drama'. (unpublished paper) London: ILEA.

Taylor, J. (1986) 'Frankenstein's Monster', *London Drama Magazine*, 7 (3), Autumn, 17–19.

Thorp, D.M. *et al.* (1995) 'Effects of sociodramatic play training on children with autism', *Journal of Autism and Developmental Disorders*, **25** (3), 265–81.

Turner, M.A. (1997) 'Towards an executive dysfunction account of repetitive behaviour in Autism', in Russell, J. (ed.) *Autism as an Executive Disorder*. Oxford: Oxford University Press.

Turner, M.A. (1999) 'Generating novel ideas: fluency performance in high functioning and learning disabled individuals with Autism', *Journal of Child Psychology and Psychiatry*, **40**, 189–201.

Volkmar, F.R. (1987) 'Social Development', in Cohen, D. J. and Donnellan, A. (eds) *Handbook of Autism and Pervasive Developmental Disorders*. New York: Wiley.

Vygotsky, L.S. (1978) *Mind in Society: the development of higher psychological processes*. Cambridge, MA: Harvard University Press.

Whitehead, M. (1997) *Language and Literacy in the Early Years*. London: Paul Chapman.

Whittaker, C. (1996) 'Spontaneous proximal communication in children with autism and severe learning difficulties', in *Therapeutic Interventions in Autism*, National Autistic Society: Autism Research Unit, Sunderland University.

Williams, D. (1996) *Autism: An Inside-out Approach*. London: Jessica Kingsley.

Wing, L. (1996) *The Autistic Spectrum*. London: Constable.

Witkin, R. (1974) *The Intelligence of Feeling*. London: Heinemann.

Wolfberg, P.J. (1999) *Play and Imagination in Children with Autism*. New York: Teachers College Press.

Wood, D.J *et al.* (1976) 'The Role of Tutoring in Problem-solving', *Journal of Child Psychology and Psychiatry*, **17**, 89–100.

Index